THESES
AND
DISSERTATIONS

A Guide to Writing in the Social and Physical Sciences

W9-CIN-009

Isadore Newman
Carolyn R. Benz
David Weis
Keith McNeil

University Press of America, Inc.
Lanham • New York • Oxford

Copyright © 1997 by
University Press of America,® Inc.
4720 Boston Way
Lanham, Maryland 20706

12 Hid's Copse Rd.
Cummor Hill, Oxford OX2 9JJ

Library of Congress Cataloging-in-Publication Data

Theses and dissertations : a guide to writing in the social and physical
sciences / Isadore Newman . . . (et al.).
1. Dissertations, Academic. 2. Social sciences--Research--
Methodology. 3. Physical sciences--Research--Methodology. 4.
Proposal writing in research. I. Newman, Isadore.
LB2369.T44   1997 808'.02--dc21   97-21779 CIP

ISBN 0-7618-0814-0 (cloth: alk. ppr.)
ISBN 0-7618-0815-9 (pbk: alk. ppr.)

♾™The paper used in this publication meets the minimum
requirements of American National Standard for information
Sciences—Permanence of Paper for Printed Library Materials,
ANSI Z39.48—1984

Contents

List of Exhibits

LIST OF EXHIBITS

Preface

The text provides an organizing format for getting started in writing a dissertation or thesis. The step-by-step presentation is intended to provide the graduate student with a clear plan for preparing the manuscript. The usual front matter is presented in a separate prologue that precedes chapter 1. Chapters 1 through 5 correspond to the typical first five chapters in a dissertation or thesis. Thus, any referencing to the chapters in the text corresponds to the same chapter in the thesis. Material normally following the last chapter is presented in chapter 6. Hints for working with the student's committee and the chair are presented in chapter 7. All material in the text is typed in APA format, and various tips regarding APA format are presented in chapter 8. The last chapter, chapter 9, contains various timelines and checklists to assist the student in planning and executing the study.

Each of the chapters contains timely tips for planning, conducting, and surviving the thesis or dissertation. Each also has numerous examples of written sections, necessary letters, and planning guides. The appendices contain numerous examples of tables and figures.

Acknowledgements

We would like to thank the following students who have given us permission to use examples from their dissertations. We feel that these are particularly good examples.

Blanchard, C. W. (1993). *Effects of ropes course therapy on interpersonal behavior and self-esteem of adolescent psychiatric inpatients.* Unpublished doctoral dissertation, New Mexico State University, Las Cruces, NM.

Burks, C. R. (1994). *An assessment of parental needs when a child is diagnosed with a chronic illness.* Unpublished doctoral dissertation, New Mexico State University, Las Cruces, NM

Cole, M. L. (1993). *A study of the relationship between site based management, teacher decisional participation, and school climate.* Unpublished doctoral dissertation, New Mexico State University, Las

Haupt, C. (1992). *Facilitation effects: Determinants of drug use among Hispanic and White Non-Hispanic fourth, fifth, and sixth grade public school students.* Unpublished doctoral dissertation, New Mexico State University, Las Cruces, NM.

Johnson, P. F. (1996). *The impact of parental divorce on young adult development: A multivariate analysis.* Unpublished doctoral dissertation, New Mexico State University, Las Cruces, NM.

Montoya, C. A. (1994). *The effects of teacher involvement on the planning of secondary schools.* Unpublished doctoral dissertation, New Mexico State University, Las Cruces, NM.

Powers, P. A. (1995). *Parental psychological equilibrium and optimal family functioning.* Unpublished doctoral dissertation, New Mexico State University, Las Cruces, NM. Cruces, NM.

Woods, E. S. (1996). *Correlates of effective mathematics problem solving among preservice elementary teachers.* Unpublished doctoral dissertation, New Mexico State University, Las Cruces, NM.

Prologue

This text is intended to be an organizing format for getting started in writing a dissertation or thesis. The step-by-step presentation is intended to provide the graduate student with a clear plan for preparing the manuscript. There is, of course, not just one way to carry out reporting of graduate research; but these ideas will help getting the effort started. While there are variations among disciplines, among universities, among departments within the same university, and among members of your own committee, the important point to remember is to get all the components in somewhere.

TIP: Review completed theses and dissertations chaired by the same person that you are considering to be your chair.

Besides digesting this text, students are encouraged to obtain two other documents early in the process: first, the current thesis and dissertation guideline from one's particular university or college, and second, a current edition of an editorial style manual, such as the American Psychological Association's (APA) style manual. The emphasis is on "early in the process" so that mistakes can be prevented; and on "current" editions of the guidelines because they change frequently. Besides the rules for punctuation and formatting, the style manual contains important guidelines for such issues as writing style, attribution of content to original authors, warnings about plagiarism, and technical directions for graphs and tables.

Writing the manuscript is not a linear process, but one in which components of the research process evolve as the conceptualization develops and becomes increasingly clear through the literature review. One typically begins with a topic, an idea, an area of interest. Tentative literature searches are conducted. Variables of interest surface, and hypotheses are stated in a preliminary way. Reflection on one's interests, one's access to data sources, and discussions with an advisor usually result in modifications of initial thoughts and plans. Components of chapter 3--such as research design and derivation of hypotheses--provide a structure to help the researcher to record the specifics of the study as they evolve. Attending to purpose statements and hypotheses helps to focus the review of literature (chapter 2), which otherwise can become unwieldy and far afield from that necessary to support the study.

Writing and rewriting are part of the manuscript process. Writing a final draft the first time is improbable if not impossible. Rather than linear, the process is cyclical. For instance, it is typical to begin with those areas required in chapter 1--the general research question and operational definitions. Next, one might go to chapter 3 to write tentative specific hypotheses. These will likely change as one reviews the literature relevant to the topic. The literature review studies are summarized, critiqued, and intertwined in chapter 2. The individual studies in the final literature review had been accumulating before the questions in chapter 1 were fully conceptualized.

This text presents the organization of the final manuscript. Though it is presented in a linear fashion, one should realize that it was likely neither conceptualized nor written in the apparent linear fashion.

Important Guidelines for Using this Text

Each dissertation or thesis is different in terms of writing style, format, number of instruments, length of the manuscript, etc. The content and format recommended here are logical, developmentally sequenced, comprehensive, and readable by a variety of audiences. Examples are provided throughout this text. Some are sections from a dissertation addressing the effects of computer assisted instruction. Others are from a fictitious master's thesis on the effects of two treatments on the reduction of bulimic behavior, while others are from various dissertations that the authors have been associated.

In this text, chapters 1-5 are preceded by a table of contents as it might appear in the actual manuscript. The table of contents serves as an outline for the sections of those chapters.

Although the examples are typed according to the APA style manual, another style manual may be required at your institution. One should obtain the appropriate local guideline and even attempt to contact the local editor early in the manuscript preparation process.

Generally, the body of the manuscript is divided into five chapters. One should check with one's advisor or the graduate school concerning the number of chapters and the required content within each chapter. Because the five-chapter format is so commonly preferred, the remainder of this text will explicate the specifics of that format.

This text is presented in a sequence that parallels the sequence of the actual manuscript. In order for chapters 1-5 to parallel chapters 1-5 of a typical thesis or dissertation, the front matter is presented in the later section of this prologue. (See Exhibit 0.1 for one example of the organization of a thesis or dissertation.) The title page is presented first, followed by the signature page, the abstract, and acknowledgements page. Next in sequence is a table of contents that provides the guiding framework for the thesis or dissertation. A list of tables and a list of

Exhibit 0.1. Organization of a thesis or dissertation.

Title Page
Signature Page
Abstract
Acknowledgments Page
Table of Contents
List of Tables
List of Figures
Chapter 1. The Problem
Chapter 2. Review of the Literature
Chapter 3. Procedures
Chapter 4. Results
Chapter 5. Summary, Conclusions, and Implications
References
Appendices

---

figures concludes the front matter. Each chapter of the manuscript is treated in a separate chapter of this text.

Overview of the Chapters of a Thesis or Dissertation

Chapter 1 includes an introduction that develops the general background of the research. This is followed by a more specific statement of the problem, assumptions underlying the study, general research hypotheses, significance of the study, delimitations, and definitions of terms.

Chapter 2 presents the review of the literature, including a review of the problem area and the instruments that measure the constructs.

Chapter 3 describes the methodology of the study including the rationale, selection of the sample, the instruments used, the specific research hypotheses, data collection procedures, limitations, and statistical techniques used.

Chapter 4 includes the results of the analyses.

Chapter 5 contains the summary, conclusions, implications of the study, and recommendations for further research.

The references and appendices follow chapter 5.

Title Page

The title page identifies the tile of the manuscript, whether it is a dissertation or a master's thesis, the university at which it was completed, the degree it was produced for, the author (YOU!!), and the month finished. Two examples of a title page appear in Exhibits 0.2 and 0.3.

TIP: If only several variables are studied, the title should name the variables.

TIP: If many variables are being studied, only the types of variables should be named.

TIP: A title should say what was studied--not the results of the study.

TIP: A title should be consistent with the research hypotheses, purposes, or questions.

Exhibit 0.2. Example title page of a dissertation.

THE EFFECTS OF COMPUTER ASSISTED
INSTRUCTION ON ACADEMIC ACHIEVEMENT

A Dissertation
Presented to
The Graduate Faculty of the University of Akron

in Partial Fulfillment
of the Requirements for the Degree
Doctor of Philosophy

Mary M. Smith
June 1990

Exhibit 0.3. Example title page of a master's thesis.

A NEW TREATMENT FOR BULIMIC WOMEN

By
María L. González, B. A.

A Thesis submitted to the Graduate School
in partial fulfillment of the requirements
for the degree Master of Arts

Major Subject: Counseling
Minor Subject: Multicultural Studies
New Mexico State University
Las Cruces, New Mexico
Copyrighted 1996 by María Luisa González
April 1996

Exhibit 0.4. Example signature page of a dissertation.

THE EFFECTS OF COMPUTER ASSISTED
INSTRUCTION ON ACADEMIC ACHIEVEMENT

A Dissertation by

Mary M. Smith

Approved: Accepted:

_____   _____

Advisor   Dean of the College

_____   _____

Faculty Reader   Dean of the Graduate School

_____   _____

Department Chair   Date

Signature Page

The signature page follows the title page. Because this is a formal page, it is very important that all signatures are obtained. Sometimes, each member of the student's committee signs the signature page. Exhibit 0.4 contains an example signature page of a dissertation.

Abstract

The abstract succinctly and briefly summarizes the entire research study. This section allows the reader to obtain a general overview of the study. The abstract should stand by itself without forcing a reader to examine the main body of the study. Components to include in the abstract are:

purpose
problem
research design
procedures
sample
instruments
statistical procedures
results
conclusions
implications

The abstract is usually limited in length (total number of words), and should be prepared carefully as it will be the primary access point for many subsequent researchers. For instance, the abstracts of dissertations are published in Dissertation Abstracts International--without revision. To initiate writing the abstract, one might first write two sentences reflecting each chapter. That is, write two sentences about the purpose, two sentences about prior research, two sentences about procedures, two sentences about results, and two sentences about implications. These 10 sentences should be a good starting point of that abstract. Exhibit 0.5 contains an abstract for a master's thesis.

Exhibit 0.5. An abstract from a fictitious master's thesis.

Abstract

Young female adults who responded to an ad for a new approach for treating bulimia were administered a pretest self-report instrument to decide if they had bulimia. Those who met the criteria were randomly assigned to one of two treatment groups--multifaceted or educational. After three months of treatment, the multifaceted treatment was found to be more effective at posttest and to have caused more reduction in the bulimic behavior of the women from pretest to posttest. The effectiveness of the multifaceted approach was observed for both Hispanic women and Anglo-American women.

While the abstract appears early in the manuscript, it is usually written last. You will find that we recommend that each chapter have a concluding summary section. The abstract should be thought of as a summary of all five chapter summaries, a kind of "super summary."

The title of the manuscript can also be thought of as a condensed version of the abstract, a succinct phrase or statement that reflects the core of the study. As such, the title is often changed at the end of the study or even during the final defense. The title is a key to the access of the study through bibliographic databases. Thus the key words it contains must reveal the important variables and perhaps the hypothesized relationships examined.

Acknowledgements Page

The acknowledgements page allows the investigator to express recognition and gratitude to those significant persons who made the final product possible. The investigator might express appreciation to (a) the advisor, (b) members of the committee, (c) significant others who contributed to the work, (d) family and friends for their support, (e) sources for financial support, and (f) those who allowed the use of their tests, materials, etc. This page appears at the beginning of the document and is usually the very last to be completed. Committee members generally prefer that it not be included until after the defense, and that is in the best interest of the student as some members may feel that they deserve more acknowledgement than you want to give. Exhibit 0.6 contains an acknowledgement page from a master's thesis.

Exhibit 0.6. Acknowledgements Page from a fictitious master's thesis.

The author would like to thank her advisor, Dr. Correct for her continuing support and professional mentoring. The rest of the thesis committee, Dr. Able, Dr. Smith, and Dr. Wesson also provided advice in a timely fashion. The author would also like to thank the University Computing Center and statistical staff for their assistance in analyzing the data. Dr. Crunchit provided invaluable service. Finally, I would like to acknowledge the support and compassion provided by my family.

Table of Contents

The table of contents usually follows the acknowledgment page. Sections of the chapters (e.g., subheadings) are indented to show levels of the various subheadings. It is not required to put all levels of subheads in the table of contents. We strongly urge students to outline their study before they even begin their literature review. The outline will change because of the literature review, but the outline will provide a road map first for the literature review and then later for the writing of the manuscript. An outline is particularly valuable because of the demands for particular information to be in the manuscript and because of the formal nature of the manuscript. Students who do work from an extensive and comprehensive outline are more organized and find that they have a table of contents already developed. Exhibit 0.7 contains a Table of Contents from a dissertation.

Exhibit 0.7. Table of Contents from a dissertation.

TABLE OF CONTENTS

(Exhibit continues)

List of Tables and Figures

Two separate lists, one List of Tables, and one List of Figures follows the Table of Contents. These allow the reader quick access to information that may be needed during the reading of the document. It is a good idea to review these lists for completeness and for parallel structure. It is much easier to read a document when all the relevant information is in the title of a table or figure and when the structure of a family of tables or figures is the same. Paging through the manuscript often does not identify these problems. Only when all the headings are brought together in one list will such problems become apparent. Exhibit 0.8 contains a List of Figures from a dissertation and Exhibit 0.9 contains a List of Tables from a master's thesis.

Exhibit 0.8. List of Figures form a dissertation.

___

LIST OF FIGURES

___

Exhibit 0.9. List of Tables from a master's thesis.

___

LIST OF TABLES

___

Style Differences Between APA and this Text

We hope that this text will provide guidance and support in the planning and writing of your thesis or dissertation. The text follows the American Psychological Association Style Manual with a few exceptions required in publishing a text.

1. APA requires only left justify, whereas this text is justified both left and right.

2. APA requires double spacing. We have used single spacing to protect a few trees and wallets. Also, left and right margins are different than APA. APA requires 1 and 1/2 on the left, and 1 inch on all the other margins.

3. In order to conserve space, the text uses a paragraph indentation of 3 spaces. APA requires 5 spaces.

4. For visual purposes, each chapter starts approximately 1/3 of the way down, whereas APA requires 1.25 inches, and your University may have its own requirement.

5. APA requires that the chapter heading be all caps, whereas this publisher requires that only the important words be capped.

Next Steps

Exhibit 0.10. The logic of a dissertation or master's thesis.

What is the research question? (Chapter 1)
What is the evidence that it is a legitimate question? (Chapter 2)
How will this question be investigated? (Chapter 3)
What was found out? (Chapter 4)
What does it all mean? (Chapter 5)

Chapter 1

The Problem

This chapter discusses the components of what is usually found in chapter 1 of a dissertation or master's thesis. The material will be presented in the same order as identified in Exhibit 1.1

Exhibit 1.1. Table of contents for chapter 1.

Chapter
1. THE PROBLEM
    Introduction
    Statement of the Problem
    Assumptions Underlying the Study
    General Research Hypotheses
    Significance of the Study
    Delimitations
    Definitions and Operational Terms
    Summary

You need to have a lot of ideas, and then you have to throw away the bad ones. **Linus Pauling**

Introduction

TIP: Never start your paper with a quotation.

The Introduction section of chapter 1 contains a brief reference to literature pertinent to the research study. Include very few references in chapter 1--only those that are essential to represent the rationale for the study. The introduction introduces the subject under study to a reader who is unfamiliar with the topic area. Specifically, the introduction presents the major emphasis and significance of the study briefly and in broad terms. It is a good idea to state at the beginning of the chapter what the problem to be investigated is. Thus, the first sentence should begin, "This study was conducted to . . ." The introduction puts the study into the context for the reader, emphasizing why it is important. It is perhaps ideal to aim the material at a person who is knowledgeable of the field, but not necessarily deeply involved in the problem you are studying. Exhibit 1.2 contains an introduction from a dissertation.

Exhibit 1.2. Example introduction from a dissertation.

Introduction

Since 1920, there has been a geometric increase in the use of educational technology to enhance instructional procedures. The success of this educational technology has been mixed. The classroom technology of the 1980s and 1990s has been computer applications. The estimate for software related to education for 1988 has been given as 500 million dollars (Smith, 1987). Community expectations have no doubt affected the computerization of many schools. There is an estimate of 60 million microcomputers in homes across the US, many of which are used for instruction or skill advancement purposes.

Computer Assisted Instruction (CAI) has become a major educational tool for developing curriculum, and a vehicle for providing instruction. Many educators believe CAI to be one of the most effective ways to improve academic achievement of students. An analysis of over 400 studies (Schwalb, 1982) has shown positive results of CAI on student learning.

Nothing is interesting if you're not interested. **Helen MacInness**

Our minds possess by nature an insatiable desire to know the truth. **Marcus Tullius Cicero**

A mind that is stretched to a new idea never returns to its original dimension. **Oliver Wendell Holmes**

A problem well stated is a problem half solved. **Charles Kettering**

Statement of the Problem

The Statement of the Problem section presents a formal and succinct statement of the problem to be investigated. It answers the question of WHAT is being done in the study. The writer must establish that the problem is an important one, and that it is feasible to research it. That is, the answer to the problem will lie in the data obtained. Speculative questions require speculative answers and thus do not meet the criteria of a researchable problem.

TIP: Pick a problem that you have a genuine professional interest in-- one that you do not have a personal interest in to the extent that you are out to prove something. Such emotional ties often blind the researcher from the resulting data.

In thinking, planning, and writing the problem section, one should ask, "What are the possible results of this research, and what impact will those results have on the knowledge base?" Answers to these questions not only provide insight for the discussion chapter, but also justify the import of the study to the reader. In addition, the general research hypotheses of the study should be clearly implied from the statement of the problem, as illustrated by Exhibit 1.3.

Never assume the obvious is true. **William Safire**

Assumptions Underlying the Study

Assumptions must be included in chapter 1. Underlying assumptions are present in every research study. Allowing them to only be implicit

Exhibit 1.3. A Statement of the Problem section from a dissertation.

Statement of the Problem

This study will investigate the relationship between the use of CAI and achievement gains in a representative sample of high school students in the US.

This study will be longitudinal in that participants will be studied at two points in time, 1980 and 1986. More specifically, this investigation will test the relationship between the students' frequency of use of CAI and their achievement gains on standardized tests and teacher assigned grades in 1980 and the amount of postsecondary education completed in 1986.

---

and not explicit prevents the reader from understanding what the researcher is assuming "to begin with." These assumptions answer several questions: What is the researcher starting with? What is the researcher's view of the phenomenon under study and the methods chosen to study it? What does the researcher believe? What does the researcher accept as knowledge or data?

The stated assumptions place the research in context. They establish the conditions under which the study is assumed to be taking place. As such, these statements protect the researcher's intentions from being misconstrued by the reader. Assumptions describe in a normative fashion what is not necessary to reference to published sources. In other words, assumptions are "givens"; there is no requirement to cite sources, although some researchers might opt to do so.

Such phenomena as societal conditions, school structures, data types, and performance systems can be assumed rather than justified with evidence. Say a researcher is investigating whether there is a relationship between anxiety and academic ability. She may assume that an IQ test score reflects the level of academic ability. This assumption is better stated than left unstated and thus unacknowledged or unclear to the reader.

TIP: State the assumptions in a series of numbered sentences, as briefly as possible so that what is assumed is clear.

TIP: In the statement of an assumption, consider stating the reason(s) why it was necessary to make the assumption. If there is a reason for believing an assumption is true, state the reason. If an assumption is questionable, consider casting it as a limitation.

The research question subsumes a particular set of "givens" based on the philosophical paradigm undergirding it. When a researcher is sampling participants from a population and testing hypotheses, there are various assumptions that the researcher should acknowledge. These include the ability to generalize from the sample to the population.

Assumptions differ from "delimitations" and "limitations" but are similar to both. Assumptions are statements of beliefs and knowledge claims within the researcher's mind. They can be thought of as internal. "Delimitations" (constraints imposed by the researcher) and "limitations" (constraints imposed by the results of the data collection process) are statements external to the researcher and more technical and idiosyncratic to the particular study being reported. Exhibit 1.4 contains an assumptions paragraph from a dissertation.

Exhibit 1.4. Assumptions example from a dissertation.

Assumptions

Several assumptions underlie this study. First, the researcher assumes that the participants investigated are a representative sample of high school students from across the country. Second, various applications of CAI technology are sufficiently generic in their relationship to learning to combine results and test CAI effects on academic achievement gains. Third, it is assumed that the self-reported demography (ethnicity, gender, and grade level) is sufficiently free of error. Fourth, the variance in reported grades is assumed to reflect random effects of bias among teachers. Fifth, it is assumed that the error in student accuracy in reporting grades is randomly dispersed.

Their real problem was that they assumed themselves able to formulate the questions, and ignored the fact that the questions were every bit as important as the answers. **Robert Ornstein**

The aim of science is to seek the simplest explanation of complex facts. We are apt to fall into the error of thinking that the facts are simple because simplicity is the goal of our quest. The guiding motto in the life of every natural philosopher should be, "Seek simplicity and distrust it." **Alfred North Whitehead**

Every great advance in science has issued from a new audacity of imagination. **John Dewey**

General Research Hypotheses

The word "Hypothesis" comes from the Greek meaning groundwork, foundation, or support. It is tentatively advanced to explain observed facts or phenomenon. A hypothesis is a shrewd guess, an assumption, an opinion, a hunch, or informal judgment. It helps guide the research methods of the study. Theory or a substantial knowledge base simplifies the development and defense for hypotheses. Hypotheses cannot emerge from nothing, there must be a rationale for each. Each hypothesis must be testable, and tested with the data collected.

The General Research Hypotheses section presents in general terms the research questions. Constructs are mentioned, not the operational measures of those constructs. The hypotheses should be derived logically from the Statement of the Problem section. A thesis or dissertation usually includes no more than five general research hypotheses. Exhibit 1.5 contains an example of three general research hypotheses from one dissertation.

Exhibit 1.5. Example of a General Research Hypothesis section.

---

1. There is a relationship between the frequency of CAI use and achievement test scores when one controls for ability level.
2. There is a significant relationship between the frequency of CAI use, instruction received, and assigned grades when controlling for ability level, SES, ethnicity, and gender.
3. There is an interaction between the frequency of CAI use and ability level in predicting achievement when controlling for ability level.

Significance of the Study

The Significance of the Study section justifies the need for the investigation. It answers the basic questions of WHY the investigation is important or valuable. One must make a compelling case for the study's contribution to the field. Grounds for the research might rest on such aspects as the emerging questions of prior studies, conflicting findings in other studies, evolution of methodologies, or political, social, or psychological trends. Most committees are looking for a one-page significance of the study, as in Exhibit 1.6.

Delimitations

The Delimitations section focuses on the context or the boundaries of the study. This section is sometimes called the "Scope" of the study.

Exhibit 1.6. Significance of the Study section from a dissertation.

Significance of the Study

Computer assisted instruction effectiveness has been investigated extensively over the past 10 years (Kulik & Kulik, 1985; Moursund, 1986; Pannwitt, 1984; Rota, 1981). However, results of reported effectiveness are conflicting. Some of these conflicting findings have been attributed to the size of the sample, the design of the study, the design of the instruction, and data analytic procedures.

Public opinion has been greatly affected by the reported successes of computers in education (NSBA Leadership Report, 1985). The recommendations of the report are influencing decision makers about how resources should be allocated.

The question that one must ask is how much of the increase of CAI use is based upon it being considered a fad, and how much is based upon outcome research showing the relationship between CAI and achievement. What is needed is an examination of the effectiveness of CAI as it relates to achievement gains in a large enough sample of students at different ability levels and for different content areas. The High School and Beyond database allows for such an investigation.

Exhibit 1.7. Delimitations from a dissertation.

Delimitations

    High School and Beyond (HSB) database was chosen for this investigation. Along with many advantages, there are many delimitations. Items measure only the degree (quantity) of CAI are used in different courses. No estimate of quality is available. The data are self-reported grades and scores on the Standard Achievement Test.

    Since there are six years between pretest and posttest, the sample is delimited to those students who were available both times. The sample does not contain participants who were mobile or not inclined to answer achievement questions.

The Delimitations section establishes the limits or parameters that the investigator chooses to include and to leave out. Examples are the population to be sampled, selection criteria, and demographic data included in data analysis. Exhibit 1.7 contains an example of a Delimitations section from a dissertation. The Delimitations section should not be confused with the Limitations section, those factors over which the investigator has no control. Some examples of limitations would be the time of day a class meets, the response rate to a mailed questionnaire, and attrition rate. Limitations are discussed in more detail in chapter 3, as they become apparent after the data has been collected.

> *Those who write clearly have readers, those who write obscurely have commentators.* **Camus**

> *In science, each new point of view calls forth a revolution in nomenclature.* **Firedrich Engels**

Definitions and Operational Terms

    The Definitions and Operational Terms section defines the most frequently used terms within the study. These words and phrases selected for definition should be chosen to be included because they will lead to a better understanding of the study. Definitions included in a research study are based on a scientific foundation: that is, distinctions are made between a constitutive definition and an operational definition. The former defines a term's meaning by using other words; the latter assigns meaning according to specific operations necessary to measure it (Kerlinger, 1986). It is especially important to operationally define terms that take on a different definition from more commonly accepted definitions that might be assumed by the reader.

It may seem difficult to decide just what should be included in the list of operational definitions. First, one could begin with the terms used in the general research hypotheses. For example, from a study guided by a general research hypothesis about gender and job satisfaction the researcher should define the term "job satisfaction" in an operational way, i.e., how it will be measured in the study.

Secondly, the researcher should note terms that have more than one definition in the literature, or are written about differently by different theorists. "Job satisfaction" in the above example has been written about by various authors. The researcher must provide the one definition applicable to the present study.

The definitions can be obtained from a dictionary or a professional reference source. It will often be the case that scholars you reference will have developed their own definition. Or, you can review the various definitions that have surfaced in the literature review, and synthesize your own definition, showing why it is more appropriate than the other definitions.

Because the manuscript is targeted to an academic audience, it is unnecessary to exhaustively define every term that a lay audience would not understand. One should keep the academic audience in mind and review the list with one's advisor to decide appropriate terms to include in this section. Exhibit 1.8 contains the definitions of our CAI dissertation example.

TIP: All of the variables in each research hypothesis, purpose, or question should be defined. Also, define any attribute of your population. Theories and models should also be defined.

TIP: If an unpublished instrument was used, the whole instrument should be reproduced in an appendix to operationally define the variable.

TIP: Operational definitions should be sufficiently specific so that another investigator can replicate the study.

Exhibit 1.8. Definitions from a dissertation.

Definitions and Operational Terms

Ability score: ability was operationally defined by the Standardized Vocabulary Test from the HSB study.

Ethnicity: the self-identification of being Black, Hispanic, White (not Hispanic), or Other.

Grades: letter grades that are self-reported by students.

Socioeconomic status: a composite score based upon factors of family income, and operationally defined as the SES score on the HSB database.

Summary

The Summary section should briefly summarize all the major areas of focus covered by the first chapter. It synthesizes the chapter without repeating verbatim what is in the chapter. The summary helps a reader, who is unfamiliar with the content area, to superficially examine the material in the chapter. The Summary section is considered optional by some committees; However, to be consistent, if a summary is used in the first chapter, then a summary should appear at the end of each chapter.

Chapter 2

Review of the Literature

Every great advance in natural knowledge has involved the absolute rejection of authority. **Thomas H. Huxley**

Believe nothing and be on guard against everything. **Latin Proverb**

These are not my figures I'm quoting. They're from someone who knows what he's talking about. **US congressperson in a debate**

As we have suggested in the Prologue, the structure of theses and dissertations differs from one committee to another. Three major differences occur with respect to the Review of the Literature section. First, how the chapter is labeled varies. Some committees want the material to be limited to data-based material, and therefore accept the title, "Review of Research." Others allow inclusion of non data-based material, such as letters, newspaper accounts, theories, etc. In these cases, "Review of the Literature" is more appropriate.

TIP: Whenever you do include non data-based conclusions, be sure to use verbs that are appropriate. For data-based conclusions, use such verbs as "found," "detected," and "resulted in." For non data-based conclusions, use verbs such as "feels," "guessed," and "has the opinion of."

Second, some committees prefer the Review of the Literature material to be part of chapter 1, particularly if chapter 1 does not seem to be able to stand alone. The prevailing preference is to have the Review of the Literature material be a separate chapter, and that is how we present it.

Third, some committees want only a brief review, expecting the student to expand on it after the proposal defense. We feel that the research can be conceptualized only after a thorough literature review. In addition, it is to the student's benefit to view the proposal defense as culminating in a contract. Such a contract can be completed only after a thorough review of the literature. Exhibit 2.1 contains a dissertation example of the contents of chapter 2, "Review of the Literature." In an actual study, subheadings would likely expand each section.

Exhibit 2.1. Table of contents for chapter 2.

Chapter
2. REVIEW OF THE LITERATURE
    General Background Information
    Theory
    Instruments
    Summary

Chapter 2 contains selected literature about the problem under investigation. There are several reasons why the literature review is important. First, the review identifies what has been done before the present study to preface the current study's contribution to the body of knowledge. Second, the review provides various approaches to gathering and analyzing data for the current study. It helps justify the approach taken in your study. Third, the review of literature helps to justify the value, importance, and need for the study. Fourth, the literature review is used as an aid in delimiting the problem under investigation.

How Is the Review Accomplished?

A major difficulty is deciding where to begin the review. The best approach is to underline the key words in the research problem statement. These key words describe the ideas of the proposed study. For example, if attitude toward females in the labor force is the focus of the study, the key words may be "labor force," "attitudes," "opinions," and "prejudices" as they relate to "females." A good starting place is a computerized database thesaurus, such as the Thesaurus of ERIC Descriptors for educational topics or the Psychological Abstracts' Thesaurus of Psychological Index Terms. These key words can be used to enter electronic bibliographic databases such as Psychological Abstracts, Sociological Abstracts, The Education Index, and Dissertation Abstracts International. Besides on-line searches, it is important to review books, journals, and other relevant documents such as annual convention programs. Finally, one would be remiss if searches of the Internet were not conducted. Each researcher will likely find several sites that are applicable to their topic. Experienced researchers are often more available over the Internet than through more traditional sources.

A first source often leads to others as one follows references. Both electronic and personal literature reviews are necessary. The former (alone) precludes chance revelations and is limited to materials that are on-line; the latter (alone) requires too much time to exhaust readily available sources. Exhibit 2.2 contains a list of sources that may be helpful.

TIP: Do an outline of your Review of the Literature section before you search the literature and refine it often.

In obtaining literature sources, one works backwards, beginning with the most recent year and working back in time. Generally, a review is limited to the last 10 years, unless a topic dictates a more thorough examination. However, if dealing with an established theory, pertinent information may come from the entire time that the theory has been in existence.

TIP: Do not try to include in the literature review all of the studies that you have read. Only include those that are relevant and necessary to your study.

TIP: If there are several studies discussed in one section, discuss them in chronological order. Express to the reader how the ideas were developed.

Exhibit 2.2. Major bibliographic sources.

---

1. Psychological Abstracts
2. Sociological Abstracts
3. Education Index
4. Dissertation Abstracts International
5. ERIC (Education Resource Information Center)
6. Cumulated Subject Index to Psychological Abstracts
7. Cumulated Authors' Index to Psychological Abstracts
8. Review of Educational Research
9. Current Index to Journals in Education
10. Encyclopedia of Educational Research
11. The Yearbooks of the National Society for the Study of Education
12. The Annual Review of Psychology
13. Social Science Citation Index
14. School Review
15. University Microfilms
16. Readers' Guide to Periodical Literature
17. International Index
18. New York Times Index
19. Medline

Because each research study deals with a different problem, the sections contained within the review of the literature vary greatly. However, it is important to consider the current and past research findings that are similar to the present study. The review must also include the literature on the various ways that the constructs have been measured. The review needs to be crafted such that the reader is lead to believe that the procedures chosen and the measures chosen are obvious choices. Once made obvious, more detail can be provided on the selected instruments, such as the reliability and validity of the instrument, particularly for the population under investigation. The more detailed information on the selected instrument often appears in chapter 3.

One way to categorize previous research is whether the statement was a result of (a) a data-based study or (b) an opinion. Opinions need to be reflected as just that--opinions. Another way to categorize research is whether it is (a) a primary source, or (b) a secondary source that refers to the primary source. You should obtain the primary source whenever possible as secondary source authors often selectively put their own slant on the information in the primary source.

TIP: When reading the literature, put quotes around material that you are copying verbatim, so that the quotation is accurate in your final copy.

Chapter 2 must be written as if it were to be published as a separate manuscript. It stands alone as a critical analysis of the topic. Two prototypes for a critical review are the Review of Educational Research and the Annual Review of Psychology. Each article is an analysis and synthesis of a particular topic, including conclusions that can be drawn from the studies included.

> *The rules of the game: Learn everything, read everything, inquire into everything . . . When two texts, or two assertions, or perhaps two ideas, are in contradiction, be ready to reconcile them rather than cancel one by the other; regard them as two different facets, or two successive stages, of the same reality, a reality convincingly human just because it is complex.*
> **Marguerite Yourcenar**

The process of reviewing the literature is a thoughtful one. Mere summaries of articles on topics related to the present study are inappropriate. It is important that the literature reviewed be critiqued openly and impartially. Each should be discussed in the present study. The investigator may want to answer such questions as:

How did the researcher conceptualize the problem?

What were the assumptions? How do they fit with the assumptions of my study?

Were the operational definitions similar to those in my study?

How were the constructs measured?

How is this research relevant to my study?

How internally consistent is the study in terms of the theoretical framework, design, sampling, data analysis, and conclusions?

TIP: The literature review should be presented as an essay--not as an annotated list.

TIP: The literature review should emphasize findings of previous research--not just the methodologies and the variables studied.

TIP: Point out trends and themes in the literature. Point out the gaps as well.

TIP: Use direct quotes sparingly, and only to make the point better than you could in your own words.

The critiques in chapter 2 may be organized in several ways-- chronologically, by topic, by type of research, or another schema that makes sense. One should try various outlines to decide which provides a better flow. The investigator should keep in mind that the intent of the chapter is to clarify how the current study fits into the total scientific study of the topic. Making sense of the background of the proposed study requires critical probing into prior research and thoughtful analyses and syntheses. After reviewing a body of literature using the above questions, use that analysis to help plan ways to address the shortcomings of the prior research. For example, one may find a set of conflicting studies, some in support of the proposed study and others opposed. Looking at the supportive studies, ask yourself, "What are the characteristics of those studies?" The same question could be posed for non-supportive studies. The investigator then should think of ways to carry out the proposed study that could eliminate those discrepancies.

General Background Information

The General Background Information section is usually the longest part of the manuscript. This section should include an organized review of the past and present literature in relationship to the problem, purpose of the study, and the general research hypotheses to be tested.

Generally, the best organization is from the most general to the more specific background literature. Most important, when this section is completed, the reader should be convinced that the background information has been organized and presented in a way that allows for a clear understanding of the problem under investigation.

The chapter 2 title, "Review of the Literature," is the standard manner for presenting the chapter; Also, the major subheadings are used for organizing the chapter or providing guidelines for the reader. A brief introduction that outlines the chapter, as illustrated in Exhibit 2.3, appears first in the chapter.

Exhibit 2.3. General Background Information section from a review of the literature from a dissertation.

General Background Information

The following is primarily a review of empirical research on computer assisted instruction. However, technical reports are also reviewed since these reports tend to be influential in effecting school policy decision making. The review of literature will be mainly focused on the relationship between computer assisted instruction and school achievement.

The chapter is divided into four sections. The first section is a historical background of the development of computer assisted instruction. The second section deals with the relationship between computer assisted instruction and school achievement. The third section focuses on experimental research dealing with effectiveness of CAI and school achievement. The fourth section considers the correlational research studies that investigated the relationship between CAI and school achievement.

Theory

Not all theses and dissertations will be based on some theory. Our experience is that if a student can base the study on a theory, the whole study will be easier, be cleaner, and will more likely contribute to the knowledge base. The theory will provide a structured background and easily place the student's research within the knowledge base. The theory will identify clearly the boundaries of the literature review. Finally, the theory will help the writing of the discussion of results and how these results fit into the knowledge base. We strongly encourage basing your research on some theory, although we also realize that many good research studies have not relied on a theory.

Instruments

This is the standard major heading for presenting the review of literature on the various instruments used to measure the constructs under investigation. A case needs to be made about why the particular instruments were chosen over those previously used to measure the same construct. This section should contain only the literature on the instruments as it pertains to the current study (population, setting, etc.). Begin the literature search by examining the most current instruments first, and then work backwards chronologically. Exhibit 2.4 provides an example from a fictitious master's thesis.

Exhibit 2.4. Example review of the literature on the instruments.

Instruments

There have been several studies conducted with the MMPI, investigating the profile of bulimic women as contrasted with normal, anorexic, and other eating disorders (Ross, 1983; Scott & Baroffio, 1985). The value of the MMPI is in the comparisons to other clinical groups. A limitation to the MMPI is that the items were not developed specifically for bulimia. Consequently, several specific measures have been developed. Garner and Garfinkel (1979) developed the Eating Attitudes Test. Garner, Olmstead, and Polivy (1983) developed the Eating Disorders Inventory. Both tests were based on the DSM–III definition of bulimia. That definition was revised by the American Psychiatric Association in 1987, and consequently those two tests do not measure the current definition of bulimia. The BULIT (Smith & Thelen, 1984) has been widely used by various researchers, and the revised version (BULIT-R) is consistent with the new APA definition (Thelen, Farmer, Wonderlich, & Smith, 1990).

The BULIT–R is a five–point Likert scale in which severity of response is suggested with a score of "5" going to the most severe response. Scores range from a low of 28 to a high of 140. Previous researchers have used scores of 104 and above to suggest bulimia, and that was the criterion used in this study. Thelen et al. (1990) reported a test–retest reliability correlation of .87. Predictive validity results were reported by the same authors as ranging from .64 to .89.

In reviewing the pertinent literature on the instruments make sure that the following information has been included:

1. The reliability and validity estimates, and

2. A description of the samples to which the instruments have already been administered.

TIP: Each variable used on a questionnaire or any other instrument should have a corresponding section in the Review of the Literature.

Summary

Get your facts first, and then you can distort them as much as you please. **Mark Twain**

The Summary section should briefly summarize all the major points within chapter 2. It should synthesize the chapter without repeating verbatim the material presented in the chapter. The Summary section allows an outside reader the opportunity to become acquainted with the review of the literature and instruments used in the study. By reading the Summary section, the reader will discover what historical, theoretical, and empirical literature support the current investigation. Exhibit 2.5 provides an example of a Summary section for chapter 2.

Exhibit 2.5. Example of a chapter 2 Summary section from a dissertation.

Summary

The review of literature strongly supports the need to investigate where CAI is most and least effective. The examination of the literature supports that the conflicting results of CAI may be due to the sample specificity, content specificity, and quantity and quality concerns. The review also supports the appropriateness of using the HSB data because of its sound development, outstanding sample representativeness, and acceptable reliability and validity.

TIP: Do not end a chapter with a quotation.

Chapter 3

Procedures

The typical table of contents for a chapter 3 appears in Exhibit 3.1.

Exhibit 3.1. Table of contents for chapter 3.

Science is simply common sense at its best--that is, rigidly accurate in observation, and merciless to fallacy in logic. **Thomas H. Huxley**

All life is an experiment. **Oliver Wendell Holmes**

"Procedures" is the standard way of presenting chapter 3, and the subheadings in Exhibit 3.1 is the usual way to organize the chapter. As an alternative to using "Procedures," the title "Methodology" or "Methods" might be used.

Chapter 3 serves as the structural framework for the data collection. It is the most technical part of the manuscript. It is definitive, concrete, prescriptive, and factual. It provides a focus for the reader on the scientific and empirical components of the study. Chapter 3 contains the information on research design, specific research hypotheses, participants, sampling procedures, instruments, variables and how they are quantified and coded, how data are to be collected, the details of the data analysis techniques, and limitations of the study.

TIP: Convince the reader that the methods you selected to answer the research questions were the appropriate ones.

The document must be coherent and consistent across chapters. Chapter 3 should be seen as the focal point of that coherent framework. For instance, the general research hypotheses in chapter 1 should be clearly reflected in chapter 3 in that the specific research hypotheses in chapter 3 should derive from them. The operational definitions in chapter 1 should be consistently and clearly linked to the data collection and variable list in chapter 3. The purpose and problem statements in chapter 1 must be explicitly connected to the prior research reviewed in chapter 2 and also the specific research hypotheses tested in chapter 3.

Similarly, the specific research hypotheses stated in chapter 3 determine the results in chapter 4 and the discussion of those results in chapter 5. Only through making links conceptually and planning the research and writing carefully can the researcher present a consistent study.

The researcher's theoretical framework dictates how this coherence is presented to the reader. For example, one's hypothesized variable relationships form a nomological network--a conceptualization of expected relationships. One such discussion is in Exhibit 3.2a. This could also be depicted in graphical form. Drawing the variable

Exhibit 3.2a. An example of a theoretical network.

The conceptual model proposed in this study is illustrated in Figure 1 and illustrates these hypotheses. . . . The single variable of teacher absenteeism has been repositioned as a single outcome variable, which reflects the hypothesized relationships of this study. All other major classes of variables in the conceptual model are positioned to illustrate the same relationships represented in the Hackman and Oldham model. This study sought answers to the following questions:

1. Is teacher absenteeism related to job satisfaction?

2. Is teacher absenteeism related to the job characteristics attributed to teaching, as measured by the Motivating Potential Score (MPS) calculated from teachers' responses on the survey?

3. Can job satisfaction be predicted by measuring the degree to which a teacher experiences the three critical psychological states?

4. Can job satisfaction be predicted by the MPS?

5. Is teachers' level of growth need strength related to their reported levels of critical psychological states, their level of job satisfaction, and teacher absenteeism?

---

relationships often helps the researcher conceptualize the phenomenon under study and identify those relationships that are eventually tested. An example of such a figural theoretical network is in Exhibit 3.2b.

As mentioned in the introduction, writing the document is not a linear process. This text is a prescription for the finished product. The sequence and organization of the finished work are the major foci of the text. Reiterating some of those thoughts about process as opposed to product is important.

Chapter 3 serves as the structural framework of the manuscript. It helps the researcher "tie down" particular components of the study. After beginning with a particular set of variables, for example during the process of defining the study and reviewing the literature, one may

Exhibit 3.2b. An example of a figural theoretical network.

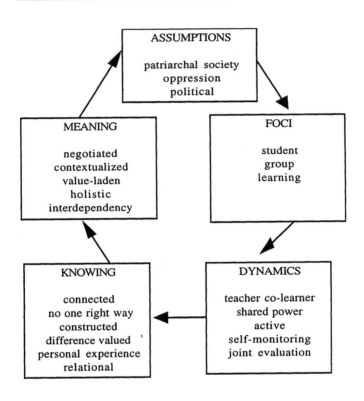

A Model of Feminist Pedagogy for Educational Administration

Adapted from Benz, C. R. (1996, October). *A model for classrooms in educational administration.* Paper presented at the University Council of Educational Administration convention, Louisville, KY.

discover that one or more of the variables are irrelevant. Variable lists may change; research design may change; and data collection strategies may change. Regarding the process, however, one does not delay writing chapter 3 until all components are in final form. Instead, one writes and expects revisions.

Research Design

The Research Design section describes the type of research design used. This section might include a diagram of your research design, using either Xs and Os, a box design, or flow chart as described in Campbell and Stanley (1963), Newman and Newman (1994), or Wilkinson and McNeil (1996). When appropriate, one should describe what internal and external validity the study had and what violations of internal and external validity took place.

The diagram of the research design illustrates to the reader the various groups, treatments, and measurements that took place in the study. If a treatment represented by "X" is an assigned or nonmanipulated variable, then it should be circled; otherwise, the X used in the diagram represents an attribute or manipulated variable. The diagram of the research design aids others in better understanding the investigation. Exhibits 3.3 and 3.4 contain descriptions of a research design.

Exhibit 3.3. Example of a Research Design section from a dissertation.

Research Design

The investigator employed an ex post facto design guided by past and present theoretical and empirical data and by specific research hypotheses. Thus, the research hypotheses were derived by both logical and empirical data findings. According to Kerlinger (1973):

> ex post facto research is systematic inquiry in which the scientist does not have direct control of independent variables because their manifestations have already occurred or because the are inherently not manipulatable. Inferences about relations

(Exhibit continues)

among variables are made, without direct intervention, from concomitant variation of independent and dependent variables. (p. 379)

Another distinction made about ex post facto research is that it contains an attribute or assigned variable that can only show relationships--not causation. Concerning research design, Newman and Newman (1994) state:

True experimental design, and only true experimental design, can show causation. Therefore, no causal statement can be made about ex post facto research. (p. 13)

The three major weaknesses in conducting a study using ex post facto research are, first, the inability to manipulate independent variables; second, the lack of ability to randomize; and third, the risk of improper interpretation due to the lack of manipulation. Newman and Newman (1994) state:

When one does correlational (ex post facto) research, causation cannot be inferred. . . . Some people have the propensity for assuming that one variable is likely to be the cause of another because it precedes it in occurrence, or because one variable is highly correlated with another. . . . However, while a correlated and preceding relationship is necessary, it is not sufficient for inferring causal relationship. (p. 122)

Although the limitations of an ex post facto design result in low internal validity, the large representative sample used in this study makes the external validity relatively high. Even though ex post facto research findings cannot be used to infer causation, the tests of relationships can be extremely useful to researchers. According to Newman and Newman (1994):

One of the most effective ways of using ex post facto research is to help identify a small set of variables from a large set of variables related to the dependent variable for future experimental manipulation. (p. 124)

(Exhibit continues)

About the type of ex post fact design used in this study, Newman and Newman (1994) state:

> There are three types of ex post facto research designs: one without hypotheses, one with hypotheses, and one with hypotheses and tests of alternative hypotheses. The first type can be highly misleading because it is one of the poorest types of research in terms of internal validity. It is sometimes called exploratory, and one should be cautious in using or interpreting the results.
>
> The second type of ex post facto research tests previously stated hypothetical relationships. It is considered much better than the first type, yet there is still the danger of misinterpretation.
>
> The third type of ex post facto research tests stated hypotheses and alternative hypotheses. These are hypotheses that propose other explanations for the effect other than the stated ones. These explanations are competing or rival hypotheses to the ones the researcher is interested in verifying. The more of these rival hypotheses that can be eliminated, the greater the internal validity of the design. However, one must still keep in mind that by its very nature ex post facto research can never have total internal validity. Therefore, causation can never be inferred. (p. 125)

This study used the third type of ex post facto research.

Exhibit 3.4. Example of a Research Design section from a fictitious master's thesis.

Research Design

Participants were recruited from two places. One was students who approached the University Counseling Center for assistance with their bulimic problem. Since not enough participants were available from this pool, advertisements were placed throughout the community.

(Exhibit continues)

Participants were administered the BULIT–R to see if they met the minimum score of 104. If they did, they were randomly assigned to one of the two treatment groups.

The educational approach is the current treatment approach of choice and is well documented in Current (1990). The multifaceted approach was constructed by the present author, and is based on the work of Ace (1990), Decker (1989), and Black (1988). The entire three months of treatment was scripted for each treatment, copies of which are available from the author. Each group met simultaneously for one hour each week. Participants were not told that they were being compared to another treatment, but were informed that after three months of treatment their bulimic behavior would be assessed.

Derivation of General Research Hypotheses and Specific Research Hypotheses

This section contains both the general research hypotheses and the specific research hypotheses that reflect the research questions being asked. Hypotheses can be confirmed or disconfirmed through obtaining empirical results from the statistics selected for analyzing the data. The hypotheses section must:

1. reflect the problems and purpose of the study

2. restate the general research hypotheses

3. state how the hypotheses are logically derived from previous data or theory

4. operationally define the dependent and independent variables

5. identify which variables are the independent variables and which are the dependent variables

6. state the level of significance (alpha level) selected, based on the concern for committing a type I error

7. state whether the statistical test is one-tailed (directional) or two-tailed (nondirectional), and the justification for the decision

General research hypotheses. The General Research Hypotheses section states the research hypotheses in general terms. The general research hypotheses, guided by the literature review, lead to the more precise specific research hypotheses. Only constructs (such as "anxiety") or general types of variables (such as "relevant personality variables") are included in the general research hypotheses. It is important to keep in mind that the general research hypotheses should clearly state which constructs or types of variables are to be used as independent variables (sometimes called predictor variables) and which ones are to be considered as dependent variables (sometimes called criterion variables). It may be helpful to set up an equation to aid in writing your research hypotheses, such as: criterion (math achievement) = predictor (anxiety) and predictor (some type of parental support).

Specific research hypotheses. The Specific Research Hypotheses section follows logically from the general research hypotheses section. The hypotheses must be stated specifically to be clear to the reader and to be testable. The operational definition of each variable must be clearly stated. Exhibit 3.5 contains several general research hypotheses and several related specific research hypotheses.

TIP: A simple research hypothesis should be as specific as possible yet expressed in a single sentence.

TIP: A research hypothesis should state what will be studied--not the possible implications of the study or value judgments of the author.

TIP: Avoid using the words "significant" or "significance" in a research hypothesis.

TIP: Avoid using the word "prove."

TIP: When several related hypotheses are to be stated, consider presenting them in a numbered or lettered list.

Participants

The Participants section describes those who participated in the study. It includes such descriptive factors as who they were and where they came from (including such information as age, gender composition, racial composition, whether they were employed, and their educational level). The conditions for participation should also be made explicit. Exhibits 3.6 and 3.7 contain examples of sections on participants.

Exhibit 3.5. Example of several general research hypotheses and several
specific research hypotheses.

Restatement of General Research Hypotheses and Derivation of Specific Research Hypotheses

There is a variety of literature that supports the effectiveness and
usefulness of CAI. If one is interested in the appropriateness and cost
effectiveness of CAI within public school settings, the studies
summarized in chapter 2 suggest that it is important to look at variables
of achievement, frequency of use, content areas, ability levels, and the
potential confounding variables of gender, ethnicity, and socioeconomic
status.

These variables, when considered, will give a better estimate of with
whom and when CAI may be most effective. That is, considering all
these variables will simplify our ability to appropriately generalize our
results.

One may assume that CAI will be more effective for students of
certain ability levels, and for certain content areas. The review of
literature also leads one to believe that it is logical to expect an
interaction between content area and ability level. It is possible that CAI
is effective for high ability students only when content areas are
sophisticated and may only be effective for low ability students when
content area is remedial in nature.

Therefore the following general research hypotheses were generated:

General Research Hypothesis 1. There is a relationship between the
use of CAI and achievement test gains when controlling for ability
level, socioeconomic status, content area, ethnicity, and gender.

Specific Research Hypothesis 1. Frequency of using CAI accounts for
variance in Mathematics Test gains, independent of ability level (as
measured by WISC), socioeconomic status (as measured by
Hollingshead's three factors), content area, ethnicity, and gender.

General Research Hypothesis 2. There is an interaction between the
frequency of using CAI and content area in predicting achievement test
gains when controlling for ability level, socioeconomic status, content
area, ethnicity, and gender.

Exhibit 3.6. Example of the Participants section.

Participants in this study were high school students who participated in a national survey (HSB 1986 follow-up) conducted by the National Opinion Research Council in 1980 and again in 1986. . . . They were drawn from a sample of 1,015 high schools across the country. . . . The investigator chose to include only 28,000 students from the twelfth grade.

Exhibit 3.7. Example of conditions for participation.

Participants were recruited from two places. One place was the University Counseling Center, where students went for assistance with their bulimic problem. Since not enough participants were available from this pool, advertisements were placed throughout the community. Participants were administered the BULIT–R to see if they met the minimum score of 104. If they did, they were randomly assigned to one of the two treatment groups.

TIP: Include a copy of your Human Participant Clearance Form in your proposal and the final document.

Sampling Procedures

How the participants were selected to be in the study is described in detail. At the proposal stage, one writes a description of sampling strategies. For example, describing whether random selection, stratified random sampling, or nonprobabilistic sampling strategies will be employed. The total size of the population and the anticipated sample size (preferably also the acceptable minimum size) is included with the procedures. At the time of the final draft, the description of how the participants were obtained (including follow-up efforts) and response rates is included. Comparison of the sample demographics with the population demographics is often not possible, but usually instructive. See Exhibit 3.8 for an example of a Sampling Procedures section.

Exhibit 3.8. Example of the Sampling Procedures section from a dissertation.

Sampling Procedures

Participants were selected through a two-stage probability sample with schools as the first stage and students within schools as the second stage. . . .

Within each school, 36 sophomores were randomly selected. See Tables 1, 2, and 3 for the frequency of special strata sampled, the number of types of schools sampled, and the number of students sampled that accepted, refused, or whose parents refused to let their child participate.

Also, the percentage of participants of each gender and ethnic group for each of the grade levels is presented.

Instruments

The Instruments section provides the reader with information about the instrument (test, survey, questionnaire, etc.). Two guidelines should be followed concerning this section.

First, if you did not develop the particular instrument, but instead used one that had already been constructed, then you are obligated to include the reliability and validity of the instrument and the reason this instrument was best suited for the study. Be sure to highlight those studies that investigated the same population as in the current study. Also discuss only total score if that is the concern, or subscales if those are the concern.

Second, if you develop an instrument, then explain how the construction logically followed from the Statement of the Problem section of your study. Show that available instruments were not adequate to examine the problem. When constructing an instrument, it is advisable to first examine it through a pilot study and report the results in this section. Some aspects to consider when presenting data concerning construction of a new instrument are in Exhibit 3.9. Exhibit 3.10 contains the description of an instrument that had already been developed.

Exhibit 3.9. Information to report concerning new instrument development.

---

1. Justification for developing a new instrument based on the research problem and purpose.
2. Procedures and methods followed.
3. Number and demographics of the participants in the pilot study.
4. The reading level of the instrument.
5. Reliability estimates and the kind of reliability.
6. Validity estimates and the kind of validity.
7. Changes made in the instrument because of the pilot study.

Exhibit 3.10. Instrument section from one dissertation.

Instrument

The survey instrument used in this study comes from the High School and Beyond third follow-up (1986). It was prepared for the United States Department of Education Center for Statistics by the National Opinion Research Center in Chicago. This questionnaire consisted of 69 multiple part questions about the student's family, employment status, educational history, income, and their feelings and opinions on several variables.

There was a total of 597 variables assessed by this questionnaire. Not all the items on the questionnaire were used in this study. Items were selected for this study that specifically related to the ideas identified by the general research hypotheses.

This instrument was field-tested to establish effective administration procedures, effectiveness of the question design, and the effectiveness of the sampling procedures (Schmitt, 1988; Sebring, 1987). The internal consistency reliabilities were all above .90 and each items' construct validity was reported as acceptable. (See Table 2.)

Variable List

When writing a quantitative dissertation or master's thesis, the hypotheses generally state relationships between variables, or differences between groups, on certain variables. A variable list, usually included in chapter 3, specifies how the researcher operationally defined the variables.

Researchers frequently list independent and dependent variables separately. If a researcher creates a new variable through manipulation of collected data (through data transformations) those variables should also be listed.

Researchers find it helpful to prepare a variable list that includes the name of the variable, the description of the variable, and the coding scheme for that variable. A coding scheme is how the various levels of that variable were represented with numbers (e.g., 1 = female, 0 = male). Explicating how the data was represented facilitates the reading of tables and comprehension of the statistical results presented in chapter 4. Exhibit 3.11 contains one such variable list.

Exhibit 3.11. A variable list from a fictitious master's thesis.

Variable List

Following is how the variables were coded in the present study. The independent variables were:

Treatment (1 = multifaceted; 0 = educational)

FES--Family Environmental Scale (1 = lowest level; 2 = middle level; 3 = highest level)

ethnicity (1 = Anglo-American; 0 = Hispanic-American)

The dependent variables were:

Post BULIT-R (score on the BULIT-R after treatment of three months; high scores indicate more severe response to bulimia items)

CHANGE (Post BULIT-R - Pre BULIT-R)

Data Collection

You can observe a lot by watching. **Yogi Berra**

The Data Collection section specifies how the data were collected. It includes the following:

1. Identifying the participants (e.g., college students, lawyers, judges, adult basic education students).

2. How the tests or data collection instruments were administered (e.g., individually, in a group setting, by mail, face to face interviews, etc.).

3. The time schedule for data collection, including period and actual dates.

4. Who administered the instruments, and the amount and nature of training in test administration.

5. What type of interaction, if any, took place once the instrument was presented to the participants (e.g., discussions between participants, discussions between participants and the test administrator).

6. Any other factors that might have affected the collection of data, such as violation of standardized testing conditions.

Exhibits 3.12 and 3.13 contain two examples of data collection sections.

Exhibit 3.12. Example of Data Collection section regarding data collected by the researcher.

Data Collection

The BULIT–R was administered before treatment to decide if participants were bulimic and then at the end of the three–month treatment. Research hypothesis #1 used the posttest BULIT–R as the dependent measure, and research hypotheses #2 and #3 used the change in BULIT–R (from pretest to posttest) as the dependent measure. The BULIT–R was administered by a trained examiner, following the test administration instructions.

Exhibit 3.13. Example of Data Collection section regarding extant data.

Data Collection

Data used in this study were collected by the National Opinion Research Center (NORC) at the University of Chicago. The data for the first of two sources used, High School and Beyond (HSB), were collected during the first half of 1980. The total sample consisted of 58,270 sophomores and seniors enrolled in 1,015 public and private schools.

The HSB data collection involved a three-day sequence between February 1 and May 15, 1980. On the first day, a representative met with the students and staff for an orientation session. During the second day, the students completed the survey and test battery. A third day was scheduled as a makeup to adapt to students absent on the second day.

An average of three hours per student was required to complete both instruments (NORC, 1980). The test battery was administered with time restrictions while the student survey was completed with no time restrictions. . . .

Answer forms were designed to encourage students to respond to each question or statement. . . .

Nearly 89% of the original 28,240 seniors completed the survey and test instruments. . . .

The second data source used in this study, the HSB third follow-up (1986) was also collected by the NORC. . . .

TIP: You need to decide what you would consider missing data and how you are going to handle it.

Statistical Treatment

There are three kinds of lies: lies, dammed lies, and statistics. **Benjamin Disraeli**

There are two kinds of statistics, the kind you look up and the kind you make up. **Rex Stout**

The Statistical Treatment section describes the various statistical techniques used within the study. In addition, the rationale for selecting a particular statistical method over another is included to justify its choice. Remember that the research hypotheses determine the research design and that the research design determines the statistical methods to be used.

As a rule, one would include the following in the Statistical Treatment section:

1. Statistical analysis techniques used.

2. Rationale for selecting the statistical techniques.

3. Advantages of using the chosen statistical techniques over other techniques (e.g., using parametric procedures instead of nonparametric procedures, testing covariance or interaction questions, investigating the second-degree relationship).

Exhibit 3.14 contains one example of a Statistical Treatment section.

Limitations

The Limitations section informs the reader about the various known limitations of the investigation. Limitations are those conditions that the investigator did not expect and over which there was little or no

Exhibit 3.14. Statistical Treatment section from a dissertation.

Statistical Treatment

Multiple linear regression (the general linear model) was used to test the specific research hypotheses. Regression models were written to reflect each specific research hypothesis. Full and restricted models were then tested to decide if the specific research hypotheses would be accepted or rejected.

An F test was used to decide if the R^2 of the full and restricted models were significantly different at an alpha of .05 for the directional hypotheses.

A power analysis was conducted to figure out the probability of making a Type II error. A small effect size was defined as f^2 of .02.

In addition, the adjustment for Type I error was employed . . .

---

direct control. Included in this section may be:

1. Research design limitations (problems in implementing the design)

2. Statistical procedures limitations (e.g., missing data, lack of meeting certain assumptions)

3. Sampling limitations (e.g., volunteer participants not completing all instruments, small representation of certain ethnic and gender combinations)

4. Testing procedures limitations (e.g., amount of time required by some respondents to fill out the instruments, difference between test administrators in spite of training)

5. Reliability and validity estimate limitations (e.g., reliability calculated on the sample data extremely low, not all desirable types of validity estimates available)

Exhibit 3.15 contains one example of a Limitations section.

Summary

The Summary section briefly summarizes all the major areas of chapter 3. The Summary section allows the reader to review the chapter's contents.

Exhibit 3.15. Limitations example.

Limitations

Although the HSB database was extensive and was supported by ample federal initiative, the data does present some limitations. First, not all of the students agreed to participate, and no analyses are available that suggest how different the participants were from those who chose to not participate. Second, some may question the "age" of the data. However, the 10 years that have intervened since the original data collection does not appear to have made any difference in the participants.

Chapter 4

Results of the Study

The Results of the Study chapter contains the demographic information on the participants and the results of the statistical tests. The interpretation of those results is left for chapter 5. Exhibit 4.1 contains the typical headings in this chapter.

Exhibit 4.1. Table of contents for chapter 4.

Chapter
4. RESULTS OF THE STUDY
Demographic Descriptive Statistics
   Results of Testing the Research Hypotheses
Summary

Demographic Descriptive Statistics

Although the population and sampling procedures have been described in chapter 3, the actual sample is known only after data collection has occurred. Once cases are eliminated because they do not meet your selection criteria or are missing too much data, then you can report the demographic information for the sample as a whole or for relevant subgroups. This demographic information helps the reader in determining if your sample is appropriate to the reader's population of interest. Age, ethnicity, and gender are often reported, sometimes because they are easy to obtain rather than being crucial to the study. What demographic variables are important varies with the study. What characteristics of the sample would you be interested in if you were reading the study? Exhibit 4.2 contains a table of demographic information from a master's thesis. Note that since there were two experimental groups that the data were presented for each group, providing the reader with the additional information as to comparability of the two groups.

Several points should be learned from looking at the table in Exhibit 4.2:

1. The word "Table" is left justified, with no period at the end.

2. The title identifies what information is in the table, how it is broken down, words of four letters or more are capitalized, and is italicized. No period is at the end.

3. A line is across the entire table at the top and at the bottom.

4. "Educational Treatment" is called a column spanner as it refers to several columns and the line underneath identifies the columns to be grouped.

5. The table note is left justified, capitalized, is followed by a period, and is italicized.

6. All lines are double spaced.

7. Only horizontal lines are used--no vertical lines appear in APA tables.

8. All statistical symbols are italicized (here M, SD, and n).

TIP: If there was attrition, state the number of participants that dropped out, the reason for attrition (if known), and information about the dropouts (if available).

Exhibit 4.2. Demographic Descriptive Statistics section from a fictitious master's thesis.

Demographic Descriptive Statistics

Participants in the two treatments were very similar on both the pretest BULIT–R (both having a mean of 110.21) and the pretest measure of psychological adjustment (multifaceted mean of 2.11 and educational mean of 2.01--see Table 1). The FES categories were not equally distributed in the two treatments (10 FES level 1, 7 FES level 2, and 8 FES level 3 in multifaceted; 7 FES level 1, 10 FES level 2, and 8 FES level 3 in educational), but the two distributions were not significantly different ($X^2 = 1.06$, $p = .58$). Finally, the secondary measure of bulimia, the EAT, evidenced similar means for the two groups. Therefore random assignment was effective for the pretest BULIT–R, psychological adjustment, EAT, and FES.

Table 1

Descriptive Information on the Pretest Variables for Each Treatment

Variable	Educational Treatment		Multifaceted Treatment	
	M	*SD*	*M*	*SD*
PRE BULIT-R	110.21	3.71	110.21	3.71
EAT	43.81	5.61	44.21	4.91
PSYCHADJ	2.01	.71	2.11	.86

Note. The *n* for each group was 25, except one invalid EAT test for the multifaceted group.

Results of Testing the Research Hypotheses

The manipulation of statistical formulas is no substitute for knowing what one is doing. **Hubert Blaylock**

Knowledge is a process of piling up facts; wisdom lies in their simplification. **Martin H. Fischer**

The investigator reports the results of the data analysis in chapter 4. Data are presented to answer the specific research hypotheses and therefore the presentation may be unique to each study. Usually both descriptive and inferential statistics are presented, and they are presented both in tabular and narrative form. The text explains the results as they relate to the original purpose and general research hypotheses.

In writing chapter 4, the researcher first decides which results to include. One may choose both tables of descriptive statistics and results of statistical inference. Because reporting research results is dictated by the specific research hypotheses, the organization of chapter 4 is driven by the design and specific research hypotheses contained in chapter 3.

After deciding what is most appropriate to include, the researcher first prepares the tables. (A variety of table formats are presented in Appendices A through G.) Each table must concisely answer the specific research hypothesis. The table must communicate on its own--it should be able to stand alone, away from the text. Then the researcher writes a narrative, describing in words what is included in the tables. At times, there may be reason to add to the planned analyses, expanding beyond what was originally planned. These post hoc analyses are presented, clearly identified as post hoc, with the rationale for the expansion of the inquiry.

Suppose a multiple regression analysis had been conducted. A report of that analysis should include the following:

1. Specific research hypotheses

2. Squared multiple correlation coefficient (R^2) for the full and restricted models

3. F ratio

4. Effect size (f^2)

5. Degrees of freedom

6. Correction for multiple comparisons (if conducted)

7. Identification of significance (S) or nonsignificance (NS)

8. Sample size (N)

9. Alpha level (α), and probability level (p)

Chapter 4 is restricted to reporting of results. No interpretations or conclusions are drawn. The narrative states only the findings from the data analysis. Detailed tables are useful for the reader, and the researcher should include an exhaustive profile of the data. One may place selected tables in an appendix rather than the main body of the manuscript. Results placed in an appendix are usually those less central to the purpose of the study. Exhibit 4.3 contains an example of a results section.

TIP: For ease in reading, report your results in parallel fashion whenever possible.

TIP: You need to report all results, whether significant or not.

TIP: Standard statistical procedures need only be named; you do not have to provide the formula.

Exhibit 4.3. Example of Results of Testing the Research Hypotheses section.

Results of Testing the Research Hypotheses

The format suggested by Newman, Klein, Weis, and Benz (1979) was used to present the statistical findings of the three specific research hypotheses. The tabled results for each specific research hypothesis include the following information:

1. A statement of the specific research hypothesis.

2. Full and restricted models used to test each hypothesis.

3. Squared multiple correlation coefficient (R^2)--the amount of variance accounted for by the model.

4. Degrees of freedom numerator and degrees of freedom denominator.

5. F ratio.

6. Effect size.

7. Correction for multiple comparisons.

8. Significance (S) or nonsignificance (NS).

9. Sample size.

Summary

The Summary section summarizes all the major areas covered within the chapter. It also must synthesize the chapter without repeating verbatim what the chapter said. This section acquaints the reader with the results obtained by the researcher. Thus, the reader may choose to check specific results for a few or all of the hypotheses tested. Exhibit 4.4 contains an example of a summary table that often helps the reader in comprehending the total study.

Exhibit 4.4. Summary table of the results.

Table 5

Summary of Hypotheses and Results

Hypothesis	Construct	Measurement	Supported
RH 1	IPB	CPI, TRF	yes
RH 2	SE	SEI	yes
RH 3	IPB/SE	CPI, SEI	yes
AH 1a	socialization	CPI-So	yes
AH 1b	achievement	CPI-Ac	yes
AH 1c	self-control	CPI-Sc	no
AH 2a	social SE	SEI-so	yes
AH 3a	SE & socializ.	SEI-So	no
AH 3b	SE & achieve.	SEI-Ac	yes
AH 3c	SE & self-con.	SEI-Sc	no

Adapted from Blanchard, C. W. (1993). *Effects of ropes course therapy on interpersonal behavior and self-esteem of adolescent psychiatric inpatients.* Unpublished doctoral dissertation, New Mexico State University, Las Cruces, NM.

Exhibit 4.5. A second summary table of the results example.

Table 22

Summary of Results of Research Hypotheses

Criterion Variable--PAFS-Q Subscale

RH #	Predictor Variable	Inter Intim	Inter Indiv	Pers Auth	Inter Intimi	Inter Triag	Peer Intim	Peer Indiv
1	Parental Marital Status	*	*				*	*
2	Overall Quality of Family	*	*	*	*	*	*	*
3	Conflict	*	*			*		
4	Cohesion	*	*	*				
5	Expressiveness	*	*	*	*	*	*	*
6	Timing of Divorce		*	*				
7	Overall Quality of Family	*	*	*	*	*		
8	Conflict	*	*					
9	Cohesion	*						
10	Expressiveness		*	*	*	*		
11	Freq of Contact	*					*	
12	Ethnicity			*				
13	Age							
14	Sex							
15	Family Structure							

Note. $N = 354$ for Hypotheses 1-5. $n = 118$ (divorced roup) for hypotheses 6-17. Inter Intim = intergenerational intimacy; Inter Indiv = intergenerational individuation; Pers Auth = personal authority; Inter Intim = intergenerational individuation; Inter Triag = intergenerational triangulation; Peer Intim = peer intimacy; Peer Indiv = peer individuation.
* significant at alpha = .05

Adapted from Johnson, P. F. (1996). *The impact of parental divorce on young adult development: A multivariate analysis.* Unpublished doctoral dissertation, New Mexico State University, Las Cruces, NM.

Chapter 5

Summary, Conclusions, and Implications

We usually see only the things we are looking for--so much so that we sometimes see them where they are not. **Eric Hoffer**

A typical table of contents for chapter 5 appears in Exhibit 5.1.

Exhibit 5.1. Table of contents for chapter 5.

Summary of the Study

This section consists of three parts; it presents a concise restatement of the problem, a summary of the basic procedures and methods, and a brief restatement of the specific research hypotheses tested. The author briefly and concisely summarizes these three areas but does not restate verbatim the material from the earlier parts of the manuscript. Paraphrasing summarily synthesizes the study. The Summary of the Study section allows the reader to briefly review the problem, procedures, and tested hypotheses. Exhibit 5.2 contains a Summary of the Study Section.

TIP: One should be able to read chapter 5 and get to the meat of the study without having to read the rest of the document.

Exhibit 5.2. Summary of the Study section example.

Summary of the Study

The chapter is divided into three major sections; the first, summary of the study, the second, conclusions, and the third, implications and suggestions for further research. The first major section, summary of the study, includes a brief restatement of the problem, a brief review of the procedures employed in conducting the research, and the specific research hypotheses tested. The second section, the conclusions, includes highlights of the major findings and the detailed presentation of each of the general and specific research hypotheses. The emphasis is on the interpretation of the significance of the research findings and what they imply. The final section discusses the implications of the findings and what further research needs to be done.

Statement of the problem. This research investigated the relationship between frequency of CAI use and achievement gain. The criteria for achievement gain was measured by four different variables:

1. Reading Test scores
2. Mathematics Test scores
3. Teacher assigned grades
4. Number of years of post secondary education completed

(Exhibit continues)

Statement of the procedures. The HSB databases from 1980 and 1986 were used in this investigation. These data were generated from a random selection of over 28,000 high school sophomores and seniors from approximately 1000 schools across the nation. Valid and reliable survey instruments addressing academic, demographic, personality, and attitude issues were administered to these students over a three-day period. The databases were made available by the NORC to the University of Akron for research purposes. Hypotheses were derived from the theoretical framework of behavioral learning theory and were tested using multiple linear regression. . . .

The specific research hypotheses. The two specific research hypotheses were:

1. There is a positive relationship between the frequency of using CAI and Math Test gains when one controls for ability level, socioeconomic status, ethnicity, and gender.

2. There is an interaction between frequency of using CAI and content area (science vs. humanities) on Math Test gains, controlling for ability level, socioeconomic status, ethnicity, and gender.

Conclusions

In the Conclusions section the investigator summarizes and discusses the findings of the research hypotheses. This section is the major focus of the chapter. It is important that the conclusions presented are only those grounded in the data-based research findings of the study. One should be able to connect each conclusion to the results of data analyzed in chapter 4. Assumptions and inferences are to be avoided in this section, but appear in the section on implications.

The researcher adds coherence by linking the conclusions to the purpose of the study stated in chapter 1 and by relating the conclusions to those studies reviewed in chapter 2. Finally, in this section one may give explanations for the findings, including suggestions as to why certain hypotheses were not accepted. Exhibit 5.3 contains an example of a Conclusions section.

Exhibit 5.3. Conclusions section example.

Conclusions

This section will be divided so that the first statements will be related to the general research hypotheses, followed by specific research hypotheses, and concluded with a general discussion of all the specific research hypotheses.

Conclusions related to general research hypothesis 1 and its 10 specific research hypotheses follow. These hypotheses dealt with the relationship between CAI use and Math Test gains for senior high students. It was found that the frequency of CAI use did not account for a significant amount of the variance in predicting Math Test gains (see Table 1). Only .01% of the variance in Math Test gains was attributable to the frequency of CAI use, independent of ability level, socioeconomic status, ethnicity, and gender. . . .

The first five specific research hypotheses (H1-H5) associated with the second general research hypothesis were tested. All these tests of interaction were nonsignificant (see Table 2).

TIP: Important strengths and limitations should be mentioned in the Conclusions section.

TIP: Avoid making conclusions that are too broad for your study.

TIP: Consider speculating on the possible effects of a limitation on the results of the study.

Implications

The Implications section presents inferences drawn from the findings of the study. It is appropriate in this section to speculate and present new ideas based on the research results. While in all of the previous sections the researcher has been precluded from personal interpretations, it is in this section that those ideas are encouraged. Here is the researcher's opportunity to suggest how the findings of the study may be applied to theory or to an organization, agency, school, or classroom. Here is where one explains the practical application of the research findings. Exhibit 5.4 contains an example of an Implications section.

Exhibit 5.4. Implications example.

Implications

This section contains the implications of the research. Based on the literature review, educators predicted that in 1991 computers would far outstrip all other educational devices in the attempt to improve student learning.

The question that this study addressed was "What evidence exists that supports the position that computer use (CAI) increases learning effectiveness as measured by objective achievement measures?" This study differed from many previous studies in that:

1. The sample was highly representative of senior high school students in the US.

2. The study was not limited to the evaluation of just one CAI program, but aggregated over CAI programs used throughout the US.

3. The specific research hypotheses controlled for the confounding variables of ability level, SES, ethnicity, and gender.

Results of the investigation showed that CAI use did not account for unique variance in predicting total achievement gains. However, there were areas of achievement gain, such as mathematics computation skills, which were significantly related to computer usage. The nonsignificance can be explained to some extent by the possibility of nonequivalently good CAI software in all the programs. This variability in the quality of the CAI software could have produced enough error variance to overpower all the effects of CAI use.

When one looks at the results with an overall perspective, that is, at how many directional hypotheses were in the predicted direction though nonsignificant, it was found that 32 of the 38 hypotheses were predicted in the right direction.

A post-hoc sign test was significant ($p < .001$) implying that there was a tendency for an overall effect and possibly that the nonsignificance may be due to variability in the individual settings, software differences, or accuracy in estimating achievement gains. . . .

TIP: It is usually inappropriate to introduce new data or new references to literature in the Conclusions section.

Suggested Further Research

The greater our knowledge increases, the more our ignorance unfolds. **John F. Kennedy**

The Suggested Further Research section allows the researcher to identify areas where future study may extend or clarify the conclusions of the present study. This section might include ideas such as the following:

1. Testing other samples from different geographical areas using the same instruments.

2. Setting up an improved research design, such as including a pretest.

3. Obtaining other reliability and validity estimates on the instruments with samples similar to the ones in the present study.

4. Examination of the treatments that took place between the pretest and the posttest to see what actually happened.

5. Examination of other variables (dependent and independent) that have not yet been considered.

TIP: If you issue a call for further research on a problem, provide the reader with specific guidance.

Exhibit 5.5 contains an example of a Suggested Further Research section.

Exhibit 5.5. Suggested Further Research section example.

Suggested Further Research

In conducting this study, a variety of additional unanswered questions arose that could be the impetus for future investigations. The following are some suggested research questions that the investigator feels would be of value:

1. Does quality of CAI programs account for variance in predicting achievement gains?

2. Is there a first order interaction between content area and gender in predicting achievement gains?

Summary

In the Summary section the researcher briefly summarizes all the major areas of focus covered within chapter 5. Because this chapter is the most frequently read chapter, it should be particularly well-crafted. Exhibit 5.6 contains an example of a Summary section.

Exhibit 5.6. Summary of chapter 5 example.

Summary

Chapter 5 began with a summary of the purpose and restatement of the problem. It was found that CAI use did not account for a significant amount of unique variance in the prediction of achievement gains. However there were specific types of achievement gains that were more influenced by CAI.

A summary of the more important findings is . . . The discussion dealt with what some of these expected studies would suggest. The implication of this study was that, at least based on the available software, CAI was more effective in certain content areas that in others. What may be needed is the integration of teacher planning with CAI use, maximizing the most effective use of this educational technology.

Chapter 6

After Parts

Material that would disrupt the flow of the document should be referred to in the document, but be placed at the end of the document, after chapter 5. Such material includes the references and the appendices.

References

The Reference section lists in alphabetical order (by author) the references cited within the manuscript. This section allows a reader to find the references cited. It is important that the references contain the following material:
1. The author(s)
2. The date
3. The title
4. If book or report, the publisher and place of publication
5. For a journal article, the journal name, volume, issue number, and pages.

All references cited in the manuscript must appear in the references. The converse of this is also true--any source cited in the references must appear in the text. Primary sources should be read and cited. One follows the same style manual for the references as for the rest of the manuscript. Exhibit 6.1 contains various examples following the APA reference format.

Exhibit 6.1. Examples of various types of references.

Journal article:

McNeil, K., & Newman, I. (1995). Going beyond the literature review with meta-analysis. *Mid-western Educational Researcher, 8*(1), 23-26.

Conference presentation:

McNeil, K., & Newman, I. (1997, March). *When the difference between two correlations can be tested by the interaction between continuous variable and a dichotomous variable.* Paper presented at the meeting of the American Educational Research Association, Chicago.

Book:

McNeil, K., Newman, I., & Kelly, F. J. (1996). *Testing research hypotheses with the general linear model.* Carbondale, IL: Southern Illinois University Press.

Personal communication:

I. Newman (personal communication, June 8, 1996)

Article or chapter in an edited book:

Merta, R. J. (1995). Group work: Multicultural perspectives. In J. G. Ponterotto, J. M. Casas, L. A. Suzuki, & C. M. Alexander (Eds.), *Handbook of multicultural counseling.* Thousand Oaks, CA: Sage.

Appendices

The Appendices section includes material that is supplementary in nature, yet inappropriate for the main body of the manuscript. Appendices are those pages less central to the purpose of the research. Whenever the material is important, but would detract from the smooth flow of the text, place the material in an appendix. The following might appear in appendices:

1. Letters sent to organizations or participants.

2. Consent form.

3. Instructions given to participants.

4. Human participants clearance form.

5. Instruments used in the study (unless copyrighted).

6. Reliability and validity estimates obtained on an instrument constructed by the researcher.

7. A specially designed computer program.

8. Tables that supplement the major findings, such as exploratory analyses on subgroups.

9. Pertinent information that would aid another researcher in attempting to replicate or evaluate the study.

Human Participants Clearance Form (HPCF)

Most universities require a HPCF to be completed by the student, and signed by the chair or department head. This form is required, even if participants are being obtained from another institution. Assurances are given by the researcher, and a brief overview of the study is usually required. The form is a reminder to the researcher to treat the participants ethically. If the participants are in any way being placed at risk, expect the form to not be accepted, or to provide a fuller description of your procedures. Exhibit 6.2 provides some helpful hints regarding your obligations in protecting participants.

Exhibit 6.2. Helpful hints for protecting participants.

It is the investigator's responsibility to decide whether informed consent can be given by the participant. It is presumed that minors and certain other protected classes are not in a position to give informed consent by themselves and special provisions have to be made for these situations.

Readability is certainly a factor. Clear but simple wording is a definite plus and serves to minimize intimidation as well as to improve comprehension.

Some researchers find that a verbal explanation prior to the participant's reading of the written form softens the impact. The potential participant must not be rushed into making a decision--you must give them a reasonable opportunity to consider whether to participate. If verbal explanation is to be given, a written script should be prepared to assure that all participants are given the same information by all members of the research team. The potential participants should be informed that The University of Akron Institutional Review Board for the Protection of Human Participants has approved the solicitation of

(Exhibit continues)

participants in the manner being used as well as the protocol of the research.

The researcher must explain what will happen to the participants in the research and what they will be expected to do. In addition, a participant should understand who is conducting the research, who is funding it, who should be contacted if harm occurs or if they have complaints.

Although it is an unlikely situation for research on campus, participants must be informed of any additional costs to them or to third parties that may be a result of their participation.

Because a consent form documents an agreement between two parties, both the participant and the investigator should retain a copy. Furthermore, the form should contain the address and phone number of the investigator and indicate how to contact the University of Akron's Institutional Review Board for the Protection of Human Participants. In some studies of illegal or stigmatized characteristics of behavior, participants would be placed at risk by the creation of certain documents linking them with the research. A written record of the identity of participants may be vulnerable to subpoena. Under such circumstances special arrangements may be made with The University of Akron's Institutional Review Board for the Protection of Human Participants for appropriate coding.

Protected classes of participants include: Fetuses and human "in vitro fertilization," institutionalized persons, pregnant women, mentally disabled persons, emergency patients, terminally ill patients, cadavers, prisoners, minors, physically handicapped persons, and economically or educationally disadvantaged persons. There are additional guidelines to be aware of when dealing with any of these populations. The Institutional Review Board can assist you in obtaining these additional guidelines.

Adapted from The University of Akron Institutional Review Board for the Protection of Human Participants

Expect about a month before approval is obtained. We suggest starting the approval process before the proposal defense, and including the approved form in your proposal. If changes are required in your study that necessitate changes in the HPCF, then submit a new HPCF, with the previously approved form attached. If changes in your study do not impact the HPCF, then you are finished with the process.

Request to Use Participants

You will likely need to obtain permission to conduct your study from another institution. Make sure that you have gone through the proper channels, documenting approval in appendices at every level. For instance, if you are interviewing all of Mrs. Smith's third graders, you will need approval from Mrs. Smith and her principal. Getting approval from the school district's central office is either a good idea, or a requirement. Exhibit 6.3 contains an example of one such request.

Exhibit 6.3. Example of appendix detailing request to use participants.

APPENDIX S

Letter Requesting Teachers to Participate

Las Cruces Public Schools
Las Cruces, New Mexico
(Letterhead Stationary)
Date
Principal's Name
School
Street Address
City, State Zip

Dear Principal:

I am undertaking a study to determine the relationship between teacher attitudes and their involvement in the planning process of an educational facility. I am undertaking this study under the direction of Dr. María Luisa González, College of Education, New Mexico State University.

The sample for this study includes secondary educational facilities New Mexico and Texas constructed within the past five years. I have been referred to work directly with you.

I am sending a packet of questionnaires for you to distribute to all your teachers. Teachers should be given a maximum of one school week to complete the questionnaire and then have it returned to you or your

(Exhibit continues)

designee.

I would greatly appreciate it if you or a member of your staff would distribute the questionnaires, collect the completed questionnaires, and return them to me in the enclosed envelope within a week after you have collected them. All information received will be kept confidential with names of respondents not utilized in the study.

As a presently practicing school principal, I anticipate that you will participate in this study since the information gained from it should assist educational administrators in future planning.

If you have any questions in reference to this research study, please feel free to contact me at (505) . . . work, or (505) . . . residence.

Your cooperation, time, and assistance are greatly appreciated.

Sincerely,

Carl Montoya
Principal and Researcher

Adapted from Montoya, C. A. (1994). *The effects of teacher involvement on the planning of secondary schools.* Unpublished doctoral dissertation, New Mexico State University, Las Cruces, NM.

Notification of Being Selected in the Study

Once your proposal has been approved, you can notify your participants. If you are conducting a survey, you might want to alert the participants that they will be receiving a survey. If you are doing research in a school, you need to contact the teachers and agree on a data-collection timeframe. A follow-up letter containing that timeframe is a good strategy and should be included as an appendix. Exhibit 6.4 contains one notification of being selected into the study.

Exhibit 6.4. Example of appendix containing notification of being selected in the study.

APPENDIX H

Request for Teacher Participation in Research

January 21, 1993

Dear Participant:

I am currently in the process of collecting data for my dissertation which is examining the relationship between site based management, teacher participation in decision making, and school climate. I am asking a small sample of teachers from all schools in the Las Cruces Public School District to respond to three questionnaires at their school site. I will meet with each group of teachers at a time mutually arranged with your principal. The completion of these questionnaires will take approximately 30 minutes total.

You have been randomly selected to participate in this project. I would appreciate and welcome your participation in this project. You are assured that your responses will remain confidential.

The time and place for meeting at your school is:

Friday   February 19   8:00am   Library

Thank you for your help in this project.

Sincerely,

Martha L. Cole
Director of Instruction

Adapted from Cole, M. L. (1993). *A study of the relationship between site based management, teacher decisional participation, and school climate*. Unpublished doctoral dissertation, New Mexico State University, Las Cruces, NM.

Script of Interactions with Participants

Variations on how the researcher interacts with the participants may affect the research results. Therefore, it is usually a good idea to have scripted all interactions with participants. Some researchers use videotapes to ensure a consistent interaction. The text from that videotape would be an appropriate appendix. Exhibit 6.5 contains a script of the videotape used to collect data in a standard fashion.

Exhibit 6.5. Example of appendix containing script of interactions with participants.

APPENDIX F

Transcript of Instructions
for the Combined Hassles and Uplifts Scales

Hello. I'm Peter Powers. As part of my research on peoples' perceptions and how their family functions, I would like you to complete the . . . If you have to stop the tape, rewind it before continuing so you won't miss any of these instructions.

Do not put your name or your sex on the form. Now look at the directions and follow along with me as I read them to you.

HASSLES are irritants--things that annoy or bother you; they can make you upset or angry. UPLIFTS . . .

When you respond to the items, you must have a specific time number on the right-hand side of the page for each item. . . .

If you have any questions about the directions for completing the questionnaire please ask the interviewer before trying to complete it. Please return the questionnaire to the interviewer once you have completed it. Thanks again for your help with this research. You can stop the tape now and begin completing the form.

Adopted from Powers, P. A. (1995). *Parental psychological equilibrium and optimal family functioning*. Unpublished doctoral dissertation, New Mexico State University, Las Cruces, NM.

Training of Assistants

If you have used assistants, you should have trained them. The training process and the process for ascertaining that the assistants had been trained can be highlighted in the Procedures chapter, and detailed in an appendix. For instance, when raters or judges are used, interrater reliability is calculated, and those data can be placed in an appendix. Exhibit 6.6 contains an example of documenting the training of assistants.

Exhibit 6.6. Example of training of assistants appendix.

APPENDIX A

Training of Research Assistants

Because 40 classes of students were in the study, four research assistants were hired to help in the administration of the norm-referenced test. The researcher first administered the test to the four research assistants. Then each of the four research assistants studied the manual of administration, and discussed their questions with the researcher. Then each research assistant administered the test to a class of students in an adjoining school district. This administration was monitored by the researcher to assure that all test administration practices were followed. One research assistant did not follow some procedures and was required to administer the test again while being observed by the researcher.

Each research assistant was then randomly assigned to 10 of the 40 classes (five comparison and five treatment). Never was any of the general or specific research hypotheses known to the research assistants-- nor did they know what treatment the class had received.

The four research assistants were also employed to evaluate the pretest and posttest essays. They were trained on the Global Assessment Procedure, and graded batches of 10 practice papers until their ratings were within one point of each rating provided by the developers of the procedure. The research assistants were neither told which essays were pretest and which were posttest, nor which were from the comparison group and which were from the treatment group.

Consent Form

You must now obtain the consent of the participants, and if under the age of 21, their parents as well. The consent form must be readable, and state what the research is about. The form must convey that the participants are not required to participate, and that they can stop any time. The consent form discusses the consequence of declining to be in the study, or of withdrawing from the study. Factors that may affect the willingness to participate should be discussed, such as physical and mental risks, discomfort, adverse effects, or limits on confidentiality.

Using your own students or subordinates as research participants is not a good idea. When you do, special care must be taken to protect them if they decide to withdraw or decline to participate in the first place. Often extra credit is offered, but equitable alternative ways of obtaining extra credit must be offered.

Monetary awards or other forms of inducing participants should not be used as participants might feel coerced to participate. Reimbursement for time and expenses is reasonable, but usually not done.

If consent is required from two or more sources for each participant, then separate consent forms are required, and they must be signed in separate environments. (No coercion should be placed on anyone signing a consent form.)

TIP: If you promise feedback, and you should, make sure that it is easy on the participants, and that the feedback is understandable to the participants. The last author of this text summarized his doctoral research for teachers. It turned out to be one of his earliest publications, entitled "Dear Teacher: This is an attempt to interpret some research findings" (McNeil & Phillips, 1968). Exhibit 6.7 contains one example of a consent form.

Detailed Analyses

Usually the raw data is not included as an appendix, but detailed analyses of the data can be included, such as ANOVA tables, or correlation matrices. Often supplementary analyses (such as means and standard deviations for subgroups) are presented in appendices. Detailed reliability and validity calculations could also be presented in an appendix. Exhibit 6.8 contains one such detailed analysis from a dissertation.

Exhibit 6.7. Example of consent form.

APPENDIX E

Consent Form

CONSENT TO PARTICIPATE IN RESEARCH

I am interested in students' attitudes about their families and significant others (i.e., spouse, lover, or close friend). To learn about these perceptions, I am asking participants to complete a questionnaire that contains statements and questions about these people. By completing this questionnaire, participants will provide valuable information about college students' perceptions of significant people in their lives. Additionally, participants can learn about these relationships by meeting with the researcher to discuss their individual results.

Your participation in this study is completely voluntary and you are free to withdraw any time. No names will be used in any phase of this study to ensure confidentiality. If you would like to participate, please sign your name below. Thank you for your cooperation.

Signature: _____ Date: _____

Principal Investigator: Rick Johnson, M.S.
Title of Research: The impact of parental divorce on young adult development: A multivariate survey.

From Johnson, P. F. (1996). *The impact of parental divorce on young adult development: A multivariate survey.* Unpublished doctoral dissertation, New Mexico State University, Las Cruces, NM.

Exhibit 6.8. Example of detailed analyses appendix.

APPENDIX R

Reliability and Validity Analyses

The survey validation process began with the initial identification of the traits underlying the questionnaire, specifically drug use and attitude. The validation process continued with item pool development, consultation with experts, analysis of the item pool, and relating the items to external criteria. Items included in the final version of the questionnaire were selected from the item pool based on data obtained from the pilot studies.

Establishment of content validity has been confirmed for this study by inclusion of attitude items designed to measure the components of value-expectancy theories. These components include general attitude, subjective norms, behavioral intention, severity, self-efficacy, response efficacy, and costs. In addition, drug use items included in the survey provided an adequate sampling of potential items concerning drug use behavior.

As evidence of construct validity, an instrument that purports to measure drug use should show age differentiation. Data in Table 3 reveal increased frequency of drug use as grade level increases. These data support the construct validity of the questionnaire based on the age differentiation criterion.

Construct validity has also been supported by the results of the factor analysis of attitude items that identified three major factors including general drug use attitude, efficacy, and behavioral intention toward drug use. Factorial validity coefficients for the attitude items were as follows: for Factor I (general attitude toward drug use) $r = .66$ to $.70$; for Factor II . . .

Construct validity has again been supported by the results of the factor analysis for drug use items that identified two major factors for each of the three substances used in this study. . . .

External analyses of the validity of the questionnaire were assessed by comparing the survey data obtained for income, grade level, and ethnicity with measures of the same information obtained from records

(Exhibit continues)

of the school district and the state department of education. . . . The X^2 tests of homogeneity revealed that there were no significant differences between survey results and district or state records for income . . . , grade level . . . , and ethnicity . . . .

Reliability analysis was conducted using the Kuder-Richardson 20 technique that explored the internal consistency of drug use items. . . .

From Haupt, C. (1992). *Facilitation effects: Determinants of drug use among Hispanic and White Non-Hispanic fourth, fifth, and sixth grade public school students.* Unpublished doctoral dissertation, New Mexico State University, Las Cruces, NM.

List of Participants

If your participants are institutions or organizations you may want to acknowledge them in an appendix. Do not identify each if by doing so some results can be tied to one of the institutions. Also do not do this if those institutions who refused to participate can be identified. A list of participating institutions, while a nice gesture, is often not included, probably for the above two reasons. Exhibit 6.9 contains a fictitious list of participants. Notice that random sampling is mentioned, and that the districts that did not complete the surveys were not mentioned.

Exhibit 6.9. Example of list of participants appendix.

APPENDIX C

List of School Districts Responding to Survey

Completed surveys were received from the following randomly selected schools in Illinois, Indiana, and Wisconsin that met the selection criteria of having built at least one new high school in the last five years (all this data is fictitious):
Illinois
   Aurora
   East St. Louis

(Exhibit continues)

Joliet
Macomb
Quincy
St. Charles
Indiana
Bloomington
Crawfordsville
Kokomo
Logansport
Michigan City
Terre Haute
Valparaiso
Wisconsin
Ashland
Eau Claire
La Crosse
Madison
Portage
Rice Lake
Superior

Pilot Study

Detailed purposes for each pilot study, results of the pilot study, and changes made in the study should be included. You should be able to communicate the highlights in the methods chapter (chapter 3), and all of the information in one page for each pilot study in an appendix. Exhibit 6.10 contains an example of detailed instructions of one pilot study.

Instruments

If the instrument used was a copyrighted instrument, permission to use the instrument should be included. If you developed the instrument yourself, then include the entire instrument. If you mailed out a survey, include the cover letter and instructions. Exhibit 6.11 contains an example of one researcher's instrument.

Exhibit 6.10. Example of appendix detailing pilot study.

APPENDIX D

Instructions for Pilot of

Problem Solving Test Instrument

Name: _____

Thank you very much for agreeing to participate in the pilot study of this test instrument. Your name will be used only to inform Dr. Hadfield who should receive lab credit.

Please use the following guidelines as you work the problems.

Note how much time you spend working these problems. You may want to look at your watch or a clock right now and note the time.

Show all of the work that you do in solving or attempting to solve the problems. If you try something that later turns out to be a wrong strategy, please do not erase it, just mark through it. Show clearly which was the strategy you found best suited to the problem and what was your final answer.

If you choose not to work a problem, please explain why.

Please turn in your work to the MLC test booth worker, and remember to note the time when you finish.

From Woods, E. S. (1996). *Correlates of effective mathematics problem solving among preservice elementary teachers*. Unpublished doctoral dissertation, New Mexico State University, Las Cruces, NM.

Exhibit 6.11. Example of appendix containing researcher's instrument.

APPENDIX A

Participant Questionnaire

Participant Number _____

For the following, please circle the best response.

Age   17-20   21-24   25-28   29-32   33-36   37-40   over 40

Gender   Male   Female

NMSU class standing: Freshman   Sophomore   Junior
                       Senior   Graduate Student

In your family of origin, the average annual income was approximately:
under $20,000 $20,000-$40,000 $40,000-$75,000 above $75,000

What best describes the dominant ethnic culture in your family of
origin?
   African   Asian Hispanic   Middle Eastern
   Native American   Western European   Other _____

What best describes your attitude toward the study of mathematics?
highly positive   positive   somewhat negative   mostly negative

What best describes your desire to teach mathematics?
   strong desire   willing   feel indifferent   would rather not

---

Adopted from Woods, E. S. (1996). *Correlates of effective mathematics
problem solving among preservice elementary teachers.* Unpublished
doctoral dissertation, New Mexico State University, Las Cruces, NM.

Follow-Up Requests

Any further contact with the participants should be documented, such as follow-up request to complete the survey. It is sufficient to state in the methods chapter that follow-up letters were sent to those who did not respond within three weeks. The actual letter should be included as an appendix, as in Exhibit 6.12. Notice that the Spanish translation is included.

Exhibit 6.12. Example of appendix containing follow-up requests.

APPENDIX G

Follow-Up Postcard

Dear Parents,
   You were given a Parental Needs Questionnaire when your child recently attended a CMS clinic. If you have not yet mailed it, please take a few minutes to complete the questionnaire and return it. Your information is important to this study.

                                                    Thank you,

                                                    Carol Burks

Estimados Padres,
   Cuando su niño recientemente asistió a una cliníca CMS, ustedes recibierion un cuestionario pertinente a sus nesesidades como padres. Si ustedes ya no lo hayan hecho, por favor llenen el cuestionario y lo manden a nosotros por correo. Su información es muy importante a este estudio.

                                                    Muchas gracias,

                                                    Carol Burks

---

Adapted from Burks, C. R. (1994). *An assessment of parental needs when a child is diagnosed with a chronic illness*. Unpublished doctoral dissertation, New Mexico State University, Las Cruces, NM

Debriefing

If you offer to debrief your participants, and you should, then the general process of debriefing should be included as an appendix, as in Exhibit 6.13

Exhibit 6.13. Example of debriefing.

APPENDIX F

Debriefing Process

The study you have participated in is designed to assess the impact of parental divorce on young adults. The study is also designed to find out which of the variables (e.g., age, sex, ethnicity, contact with noncustodial parents) affects postdivorce adjustment.

If you would like further information about the research in which you just participated or want to discuss any feelings related to the completion of the questionnaire, please contact the researcher. I can be contacted at the Counseling and Educational Psychology Department in O'Donnell Hall or at the numbers listed below. Again, thank you for your participation.

Rick Johnson   home 646-****
                        office 646-****

From Johnson, P. F. (1996). *The impact of parental divorce on young adult development: A multivariate survey.* Unpublished doctoral dissertation, New Mexico State University, Las Cruces, NM.

Permission from Publisher

Permission to use instruments or programs that are not widely available should be obtained. The permission letter should then be included as an appendix, as in Exhibit 6.14.

Exhibit 6.14. Example of permission letter from a publisher.

APPENDIX H

Permission to use Instrument

Dear Ms. Burks:

You have my permission to reproduce and use the Index in your research. As I mentioned, it may have been translated into Spanish before but, if so, I cannot find the reference at present.

Best wishes to you in your research. I would be interested in hearing the results of your use of the Index.

Sincerely Yours,

XXXXX, Ph. D.
Associate Research Specialist

Adapted from Burks, C. R. (1994). *An assessment of parental needs when a child is diagnosed with a chronic illness*. Unpublished doctoral dissertation, New Mexico State University, Las Cruces, NM

Institutional Agreement to Conduct Research

Besides obtaining permission to conduct research from your own university, permission needs to be obtained from the institution where the participants are. The participants may be in one college at your university, in one school district, or in a mental health agency. Often state, regional, or national organizations are called upon to provide member lists, and their permission should be obtained and documented in an appendix, as in Exhibit 6.15. Note that in this case that the researcher was the Director of Instruction in the school district, but she still went through all the proper channels to obtain permission.

Exhibit 6.15. Example of letter from institution agreeing to conduct research.

APPENDIX G

Letter of Agreement for Research

September 30, 1992

Mrs. Martha Cole
Director of Instruction
Las Cruces Public Schools
505 South Main
Las Cruces, NM 88004

Dear Mrs. Cole

This letter is in response to your request to complete your doctoral research on site based management and teachers' decision making in the Las Cruces Public Schools. Since the district is in its third year of site based management, your research will provide us with information on the effectiveness of shared decision making. You have permission to conduct your research with the teachers identified for your study.

I look forward to hearing about the results of your research.

Sincerely,

Jesse Gonzales
Superintendent

Adapted from Cole, M. L. (1993). *A study of the relationship between site based management, teacher decisional participation, and school climate*. Unpublished doctoral dissertation, New Mexico State University, Las Cruces, NM.

Chapter 7

Proposal Defense and Final Defense

Before the Oral Defense

Much planning goes into any research endeavor, and most research requires all the steps to be in place. We think that grouping these steps often helps the novice researcher. All these topics were discussed in previous chapters--what is presented here are the planning aspects of these topics--the background activities that must occur but usually do not get included in the document. These steps are also included in the checklist in chapter 9. The way that we have grouped the steps before the oral defense is as follows: 1) your chair, 2) your committee, 3) participants, 4) treatment or independent variables, 5) outcome measures, and 6) data analyses.

TIP: Rough out chapters 4 and 5 before the proposal defense and look to permissible conclusions; ask, "Does the design and data support the conclusions?"

Your Chair

Which faculty person you choose as your chair is a crucial decision, and should not be made in haste. As with any decision, there are many variables to consider. Interest and expertise in your topic is high on the list. So are availability and concern for your progress. Respect within the department and the college is also important. Experience in guiding previous students through the process is invaluable. Obviously all these qualities seldom exist in any one individual. Student needs also vary, resulting in some chair attributes being more crucial. Remember that this is your decision and that it affects you much more than it does the chair, or anyone else.

TIP: A doctoral student was once overheard to say: "I did not choose Dr. X as my chair, though he is nationally recognized in my field. I choose Dr. Y because I knew that his goal was for me to produce a quality product and to finish in a timely fashion."

Your chair usually receives credit for guiding the thesis or dissertation. Therefore, you have a right to some of your chair's time. You need to discuss aspects of your proposed study, consider various options, and together evaluate their utility. Your chair can probably guide your decisions as to the composition of the rest of the committee. Your chair may know of someone's expertise, or more likely, someone's animosity toward someone else, and guide your choices accordingly.

TIP: Try to set up a weekly or biweekly meeting with your chair. Such a schedule will keep both of you motivated toward completing the proposal.

TIP: Get your chair's approval of the entire proposal before setting the defense date.

Your Committee

If Columbus had had an advisory committee he would probably still be at the dock. **Arthur Goldberg**

You will discover that some committee members will take a more active role in your proposal than will others. This may be because of their student orientation, their interest in your particular study, or their expertise that you need. For instance, most committees have a statistics and research methodology member. Most members will defer statistics and research methodology issues to that person. Since these topics cover most of chapters 3 and 4, this one person is a crucial member.

When you discuss your study with each member, try to distill it down to the essentials for that member. Ask for each one's advice in their area of expertise. Try to avoid conflicts between committee members; work such conflicts out before the oral.

TIP: If you insist on using an advisory committee (such as a panel of experts besides your committee), get their input before going to your proposal meeting. Using them after your proposal has been approved may cause problems with your real committee.

Setting a meeting time is often one of the most frustrating activities. Finding an open time for all of the committee can be difficult. You do not want to pick one time and then check to see if all will be available then. We suggest using an approach such as the one in Exhibit 7.1 First cross out the times that you and your advisor cannot meet. Then share the form with each of the other members. You need to identify the one common time quickly, as other commitments will occur.

TIP: Do not have more than the minimum number of members on your committee, for the above reason.

Provide a quality document to each committee member with a memo showing the date, time, and location of the defense. We recommend that the document be bound, either with a spiral binding or three-hole punched. Stapled or hot-glued documents are difficult to handle, and often come apart.

TIP: You are among people who want you to succeed. They are not trying to sink your ship, since you have put much professional effort into the proposal.

TIP: Before the proposal defense, review all decisions made to develop the proposal. Be sure that you can defend those decisions, without being defensive.

Exhibit 7.1. One scheduling process.

To: Committee members for Rick Johnson
From: Keith McNeil
Re: Open time for Dissertation Defense
Date: December 12, 1995

Please cross out the times that you cannot meet, and return through
campus mail. Rick will verify the meeting time.

Mon Jan 22	Tues Jan 23	Wed Jan 24	Thurs Jan 25	Fri Jan 26
8-9	8-9	8-9	8-9	8-9
9-10	9-10	9-10	9-10	9-10
10-11	10-11	10-11	10-11	10-11
11-12	11-12	11-12	11-12	11-12
1-2	1-2	1-2	1-2	1-2
2-3	2-3	2-3	2-3	2-3
3-4	3-4	3-4	3-4	3-4
4-5	4-5	4-5	4-5	4-5

Mon Jan 29	Tue Jan 30	Wed Jan 31	Thurs Feb 1	Fri Feb 2
8-9	8-9	8-9	8-9	8-9
9-10	9-10	9-10	9-10	9-10
10-11	10-11	10-11	10-11	10-11
11-12	11-12	11-12	11-12	11-12
1-2	1-2	1-2	1-2	1-2
2-3	2-3	2-3	2-3	2-3
3-4	3-4	3-4	3-4	3-4
4-5	4-5	4-5	4-5	4-5

Participants

Make sure that your sample will, in fact, be available to you. Obtaining the required institutional permission before the defense is highly advisable. Most universities require some form of human participants clearance. If your sample is coming from a school or other institution, you will need to get the approval of that institution as well. Having the university's approval in hand may speed up the latter approval.

TIP: Expect at least one month to obtain approval.

TIP: Include approval forms or letters as appendices.

Remember that your view of the study is very different from that of the participants. You need to have others read over your consent form, your instructions to participants, whatever demographic information you are collecting, and instruments that you have developed. Your chair is one good resource for such reviews. A fellow student who can be critical of your work is another source. The ultimate test is to pilot the procedures and instruments with several participants. Interview them afterwards regarding their perceptions regarding the research, whether they understood the consent form, and what they felt about the instruments. If major changes are made, a second pilot would be in order. Most committees will be impressed with the care you have taken to ensure that the participants both understand what they are to do, and can do what you want.

TIP: The reading level of the consent form should be at or below the reading level of the participants. One of us once reviewed a proposal researching fifth-graders of low reading ability. The consent form was at the twelfth-grade level! Parents and students were to sign the form in each other's presence. Most of the children and some parents would not understand the consent form. Furthermore, since parent and child would be signing in each other's presence, one or the other might feel pressure to sign, "just because" the other signed. Their signatures on the form would thus not be legal. The researcher would not have obtained their consent, although there was a signature!

Treatment or Independent Variables

Whatever you are studying needs to be supported in the literature, and described in your literature review chapter. If you are researching, say, a new curriculum, or a new way of counseling, or a new administrative approach, then you need to document why you believe that it will help the participants more than the current procedure. There is no ethical defense for testing out a "hunch," or "let's see if this is any better." Put yourself in the position of the participants and ask, "Would I submit to a life-threatening operation if I knew that the surgeon was using a procedure that was just dreamed about last night?"

If you are looking at the difference between already existing groups, realize first that no causal conclusions can be made. Second, there needs to be a reason for making those comparisons, other than, "It was easy to obtain the gender of the participants and therefore gender differences were investigated." Just because a variable is easy to obtain does not mean that it is theoretically or empirically relevant.

The treatment or independent variables that emerge from the literature review must be implementable. That is, you must be able to administer the treatment. Either you become skilled in administering the treatment, or you train others, or you rely on already-trained implementors. Similarly, if already existing groups are of interest, then you need to make sure that you can obtain or identify those groups. A treatment group is of very little use without a comparison group. Researching the difference between sexually active students and those who are not requires that you identify (within some small magnitude of error) members of both groups.

Outcome Measures

The outcome measures you are using need to be supported in the literature, and described in you methods chapter. You need to make sure they are available and that you can afford to purchase them (and purchase the scoring if required).

TIP: Often a written request to the publisher indicating that the materials will be used for student research will result in reduced cost.

Make sure that the instruments can be administered to the sample. If you are going to administer the outcome measures yourself, practice administering the measures on a similar sample. If you are relying on others to obtain the data, make sure that they can administer the outcome measures. Take the measures yourself, and watch others administer and take the measures. Debrief those who pilot your instruments.

Data Analyses

First, make sure that you are collecting all the data identified in the research hypotheses. Second, plan the analyses as to who will do them, what process will be used (e.g., computer or hand, parametric or nonparametric), and what the resulting tables will look like. While these aspects are not included in chapters 1-3 for the proposal defense, these aspects do impinge on the methods chapter, chapter 3. For instance, if no one on your committee can help you with a factor analysis, then you either find a free resource, pay someone, or spend much time doing a lot of very complicated reading.

Most students use computerized statistical packages to analyze their data. Do you have the expertise to use the computer package? Can you interpret the output? Have you designed your instruments to simplify data entry?

TIP: Even if you pay someone to do your data analysis, you will still be held accountable for understanding the results and how they relate to the knowledge base.

You are going to have to present summaries of your data in chapter 4. We have found that many students reach this point and then realize that there are additional research hypotheses that they are interested in-- other comparisons between groups, or other ways to slice the treatment and comparison groups to investigate possible interactions. Why not produce table shells before your proposal defense and possibly discover these interesting hypotheses in time to state them before data collection so that they can carry more weight than just "additional, after the fact" analyses? A table shell may contain no data, or fake data (to figure out spacing), but does contain meaningful row and column headings. See Exhibit 7.2 for an example of a table shell with no data, just meaningful headings.

Such a table shell can identify not only additional ways to slice the data, but also necessary categorizations of variables--income being a good example. Most respondents will not want to divulge their precise income (some do not even know their precise income, even to the nearest thousand or five thousand). Thus you will usually see categories of income on most questionnaires, as in the following:

__ $0 -- $9,999
__ $10,000 -- $19,999
__ $20,000 -- $29,999

Exhibit 7.2. Example of table shell.

Table 1

Means and Standard Deviations on Pretest Variables and Posttest Variables by Group and Income Level

---

	Low Income ($<\$30,000$)		High Income ($>\$30,000$)	
	M	*SD*	*M*	*SD*
Treatment Group				
Variable				
Pretest Mathematics	xx.xx	x.xx	xx.xx	x.xx
Pretest Motivation	x.xx	x.xx	x.xx	x.xx
Posttest Mathematics	xx.xx	x.xx	xx.xx	x.xx
Posttest Interest	x.xx	x.xx	x.xx	x.xx
Posttest Grades	x.xx	x.xx	x.xx	x.xx
Comparison Group				
Pretest Mathematics	xx.xx	x.xx	xx.xx	x.xx
Pretest Motivation	x.xx	x.xx	x.xx	x.xx
Posttest Mathematics	xx.xx	x.xx	xx.xx	x.xx
Posttest Interest	x.xx	x.xx	x.xx	x.xx
Posttest Grades	x.xx	x.xx	x.xx	x.xx

___ $30,000 -- $39,999
___ $40,000 -- $49,999
___ $50,000 and above
But if you are only interested in comparing two groups, those who make at least $30,000 and those who make less, you only need two categories:
___ less than $30,000
___ $30,000 or more

Requiring respondents to respond to the more detailed breakdown requires excess time, more concentration on their part, and you are not using the detailed information--all three unethical research activities. Creating a table shell for income should identify the impending problem and provide guidance in revising your instrument.

Including table shells in the proposal is not required, but it would show to the committee that you have extended your plan to the reporting of results--you have it together. Additionally, such tables often provide an organizer for the committee to understand the need for certain variables, or how the variables are going to be used.

During the Oral Defense

Materials

You should contact each committee member to make sure that they have received the document, and to remind them of the meeting time and place. This contact can also lead to the clarification of the study, or to alerting the student as to a member's particular concern. When you begin the defense, you can assume that each has read your document. You probably will be asked to make a short presentation, which has a twofold purpose. First, it is intended to reduce your stress (you start with a presentation that you have orchestrated and practiced). Second, it provides an organizer for those who have read the document and an overview for those who have not.

TIP: There may be a committee member who has not thoroughly read your proposal. Handle uninformed questions very tactfully, especially if a more careful review of the proposal would have answered the question.

Many candidates simply refer the audience to particular pages in the document. Others provide a handout of the crucial pages, along with instruments. Information can also be on the blackboard or on butcher paper taped onto the walls. Pictures of proposed apparatus can be enlightening.

TIP: Do not bring in revisions that exceed a page or two. A totally revised chapter 1 was once brought in and distributed to the shocked committee.

TIP: If have several handouts, use different colors for each.

TIP: Sit in on others' proposal defenses if possible.

Presentation

You will likely be asked to provide a short (10-20 minute) overview of your study. Focus on the highlights and possibly confusing parts of your document. You can not cover it all. Leave some material for your committee to cover in their questions. There are three general procedures for making the presentation--choose the one that fits your needs and especially one that you feel comfortable with.

One can use an overhead projector or computer presentation software. The advantage of this procedure is that it forces you to organize your thoughts and it structures your presentation. Such a presentation often presents the material in a different way than in the document--a benefit if not overdone or confusing.

TIP: Use only a few overheads or frames. Do not be totally dependent on them for your presentation.

The "essence" of the study can be placed on the blackboard or on butcher paper, as in Exhibit 7.3. The advantage of this procedure is that the "essence" is always in front of the committee--one does not have to search for the relevant information.

Exhibit 7.3. Essence of the study.

Design of the study					Hypotheses	Instruments
Group 1	R	O1	Xt	O2	RH1 The treatment will produce a greater gain	O1 = SAT
Group 2	R	O1	Xc	O2	than the comparison.	O2 = SAT
Group 3	R		Xt	O2	(O2 - O1) for Group 1 will be greater than Group 2.	
Group 4	R		Xc	O2		
Group 5	R	O1		O2	RH2 Treatment will produce higher posttest scores than comparison. (O2) for Group 3	
Group 6	R			O2	will be greater than (O2) for Group 4.	

The third procedure is to talk your way through the entire document, referring the committee to crucial pages in the document. Many candidates use this procedure as the committee (and the candidate) is not burdened with additional material.

Presenting aspects of the study in a new way can provide insight. Figures and flow charts can be particularly helpful, even if they are not in the document. Exhibit 7.4 provides a step-by-step process for selecting participants in one study. Presenting the process in such bare-bones fashion can clarify misconceptions. Exhibit 7.5 provides two ways to pictorially present one study design. Presenting pictorial information in Exhibit 7.5 verbally would be more difficult and probably less communicative to most people in a meeting.

TIP: Be familiar with the room and any equipment that your are going to use.

TIP: Topics to avoid in an oral: politics, religion, gender, handedness, etc.

TIP: Make available copyrighted instruments (since you cannot include them as an appendix).

TIP: Try to limit the presentation to 15 minutes. Discuss with chair the length of the presentation and what you tend to emphasize and omit.

TIP: If use overheads, keep in order so you can find a particular one when requested.

TIP: Practice your presentation--especially the beginning so that you get off to a good start.

TIP: Communicate an air of confidence.

Exhibit 7.4. Process for selecting participants.

---

1. Contact instructors of first- and second-year Educational Psychology classes.
2. Inform students of study.
3. Request students to fill out consent form.
4. Omit students over age 35.
5. Omit students who are married.
6. Omit students who leave blank more than two demographic items.
7. Omit students who do not provide valid pretest.
8. Omit students who do not provide valid posttest.

Exhibit 7.5. Two possible study design presentations.

Exhibit 7.5a. The study design presented in tree format.

```
         Anglos                              Hispanics
       /      /                             /       /
     M       F                            M        F
   (n=30)  (n=30)                    _____  _____
                                    /       / /            /
        acculturation            low    high low        high
                               (n=15) (n=15) (n=15)    (n=15)
```

Exhibit 7.5b. The study design presented in boxed format.

Anglo Male	Hispanic Male	Hispanic Male
n = 30	low acculturation	high acculturation
	n = 15	n = 15
Anglo Female	Hispanic Female	Hispanic Female
n = 30	low acculturation	high acculturation
	n = 15	n = 15

Fielding Questions

After the candidate has made a brief presentation of the study, the committee members begin their individual questioning. Questions are usually for clarification, or for resulting in a better study. The key is for the candidate to maintain composure and to answer the questions professionally. The best answer to any question is, "I considered that option, but decided not to include that option because . . ." When the candidate can provide a well-thought-out rationale, the question is usually settled. The more that the candidate has discussed the study with various persons, the more likely various options have been discussed, and a rationale is available.

Invariably an option will be identified that has not been considered. Then, the candidate must simultaneously comprehend the option, consider its inclusion, and consider the impact of including the option on the remainder of the study. You do not want to ignore all options, but you also do not want to give blanket acceptance to all new ideas. (Some ideas will be off the wall, or will be the pet approach of one member, and not be of concern to any of the other members.) A good chair will quickly identify good suggestions, and will quickly seek consensus from other committee members when a bad suggestion is made.

You do not want to be taking detailed notes during the oral. Try to get your chair to perform that function, or a colleague allowed to observe the defense. It is much better to have the chair take notes, as at the end of the meeting the chair can summarize changes that will be made in the study (omitting those that had the blessing of only one member).

There are three basic ways that the questioning can be conducted. One way is to have each member take turns and ask all of their questions at once. One advantage for the candidate is that you can focus on that one member, and when the questioning is finished by the one member, you can focus on another. What this means, though, is that you go through the entire document once for each member.

A second way is to go through the questioning one chapter at a time, thus bringing closure to each chapter in order. This way also allows various members to ask questions, and thus one person is not last on all questions. One disadvantage is that at times a member may "piggyback" onto another member's question and the questioning may get out of hand.

The third way of questioning is questioning from any member on any aspect of the document. This can be very confusing to the student, and is usually disruptive and counterproductive in the end.

A good chair will establish the questioning procedure, and will keep the committee on track when they deviate. A good chair will also quickly decide when the questioning is redundant, out of order, or just confusing. You do not want the chair to answer the questions for you--it is your study and you need to defend it. But the chair knows the defense process, and the other committee members better than you do. Let the chair use that information when it can be of assistance to you.

Deciding on Changes

TIP: Do not be surprised when your committee makes changes in your proposal.

TIP: The proposal is a contract between you and the committee. You (and they) must have special permission to change any part of it.

At the end of the proposal defense, a decision needs to be made about whether the study can go on. It is the chair's responsibility to suggest that the study go on, given the changes agreed upon. Usually a promise is made to provide the list of changes in memorandum form to the committee. The changes are reiterated at this time.

Some studies are poorly planned, poorly defended (remember that this is a defense), anticipated by the committee to be too difficult to conduct, or have a fatal flaw. The proposal may be rejected and the candidate asked to develop a new or revised one. If you keep your chair and your critical committee members informed of your study, this outcome should not occur.

Try to make sure that you understand the required changes. Try to identify the impact on the study of each change. Does the change increase the cost of the study such that it is not possible to complete? Does the change mean that it will take extra years (that you do not wish to commit) to complete? Since you know your study better than the committee, and since they are not overly concerned about the cost and time to you, you are the one who needs to make sure that the changes can be carried out.

Collegiality

We end this section by reminding you that the two oral meetings are two of the few times that you will sit with a group of faculty members to discuss research. You are approaching equality with your committee, and it is their job to mentor you to that equality.

For instance, once you have successfully defended your dissertation, you are on par with your committee (with respect to degree). Each may have more experience and may have more knowledge in certain areas, but you should know more than anyone about your topic and how it relates to the knowledge base. You have arrived, and but for the mundane activities following the successful dissertation defense (described in the next section), you are done, thank you doctor!

After the Proposal Defense

Now that you have successfully defended your study, you have a contract with your committee to do the study. We have divided the next steps into the following sections: administrative tasks, data, completing your document, preparing for the final defense, final defense, and following the final defense

Administrative Tasks

There are three administrative tasks that need to occur immediately after the successful proposal defense. These include documenting the agreed-upon changes, enlisting participants, and obtaining multiple copies of your instrument(s).

Documenting the agreed-upon changes. As we concluded in the previous section, there will invariably be changes identified by your committee. Some of these changes you must make, and some you will have the option of making. Once you have made these decisions, you need to briefly describe them in a memorandum to your committee. Then you need to incorporate them into your first three chapters. We suggest doing this at this time, as you must do it eventually. The other advantage of revising the first three chapters right away is that you may discover that some changes are either problematic or just do not make sense. Better to discover this now and make adjustments before collecting the data.

Enlisting participants. It has likely been some time between when you first arranged for participants and now when you are ready to obtain data from them. Thus you need to alert the institution that you are ready to conduct the study. Remember that others will not be as interested as you in your study and will not be aware of your time line and your needs. You need to remind those that play some pivotal roles in your study that you are ready to do the study.

Obtain multiple copies of the instruments. Now that your committee has approved your study, you can go on to obtain the necessary copies of your instrument(s). Two of the likely changes required by your committee are to (a) increase the minimum number of participants, and (b) change the instrument--usually just the nature of the demographic information. Both changes suggest not making multiple copies until those decisions have been completed.

You also need to keep in mind that obtaining multiple copies usually means that there is a cost involved, and that you are probably relying on someone to provide those multiple copies (whether a photo-reproduction facility or a publisher). Whenever control of the study leaves you, there is a possibility of delay or error. Therefore, you want to be the one to do this activity whenever possible.

Data

"Data" is a very simple word but it is at the heart of research. It is also where many problems occur. Part of the reason that problems occur here is that students often have to rely on others to help them with the various aspects of obtaining and analyzing data. The issue of control is apparent here again. We recommend that the student remain in control of as many data activities as possible. Some students view these activities as mundane, like typing. But most professionals now do their own typing. Even if you do have assistance in any of the data tasks, you will still be responsible for their quality, and for understanding them when questioned in the final oral. These issues lead us to recommend taking as active a part as possible in the data tasks.

Collect data. Keep in mind that people who are providing you data are doing you a favor. They do not have to provide you their data. Obtain the data professionally and safeguard it. If you promised anonymity--and you probably did--make sure that your data collection, data storage, data analyses, and data reporting all respect that promise.

Expect the unexpected during data collection. Whoever collects the data will likely be required to make many on-the-spot decisions, and that is another reason you need to be present during data collection. Document those decisions--noting the participant's identification number if possible and appropriate.

Code and enter data. Transforming information for computer analysis is usually a tedious task, but is one that requires many decisions and one that often can yield insight. No matter how often and thoroughly you pilot an instrument, someone will find a problem or do something unexpected. How that response is coded needs to be decided. Do you omit that participant? Do you omit that item? These are decisions that only you (often with your chair) can and should be making.

Develop a master coding sheet that shows how each piece of information will be transformed into a number.

TIP: If you have developed your own instrument, use a blank one for the master coding sheet. The master coding sheet will help in using the same numbers to represent the same response. Also, it will simplify interpretation of computer printouts.

We also recommend that students enter their own data. Why? Because it doesn't really take that much effort, and you might discover some anomalies in the data. One respondent might have misread the instructions, and you can make the appropriate adjustments. Often respondents will write comments on an instrument that can provide insight about how to go on with adjustments. Finally, you might discover problems with a particular item. By focusing on the pattern of responses, it may become clear that some respondents misread a particular item.

Analyze data. Again, we recommend that the student take as active role in analyzing the data. Computer statistical packages, such as SAS, SPSS, and BIMED facilitate such analyses. You are going to have to defend these analyses to your committee, so you might as well do them yourself.

TIP: Make some preliminary runs on the data to make sure that the data for each variable (a) falls within the allowable ranges (no IQ scores of 555), (b) is distributed reasonably, (c) has reasonable means and standard deviations, and (d) is correlated in the approximately correct ways with the other variables.

TIP: SAS procedures MEANS, FREQ, and CORR produce the above

information.

Only after you are convinced that the data have been entered correctly should you start analyzing the data in terms of answering the research hypotheses.

Completing the Document

Once the data have been analyzed, you are ready to construct tables, write the results chapter (chapter 4), write the discussion chapter (chapter 5), and write the abstract.

Construct tables. A well-designed table can be a great aid to communicating results. Make sure that it is not too detailed, and that the structure responds to the purpose of the table. Usually at least one table of demographic information about the sample is included. Then you can report one table for each hypothesis, or if it makes sense to group some hypotheses, one table can contain the results for a group of hypotheses. Appendices A through G provide examples. Try various configurations before settling on the one that does the best job of reporting the results of your hypotheses. Ask others to review your tables, including your chair.

Write the results chapter (chapter 4). We find that it is easiest to construct all of the tables and figures first and then write the prose. Also, place the demographic information first, followed by the hypotheses in order. Finish the chapter with a summary of all the hypotheses. This summary table will be different from the other tables in that it will convey the general results of the analyses (Exhibit 4.4 provided one such summary table).

Almost every student does not allow enough time to complete this chapter and the following chapter. Allow at least two weeks of dedicated concentration. Put the draft down and return to it later to see if it makes sense (try to read it as a committee member would).

Write the discussion chapter (chapter 5). Since not all of the results will turn out as you anticipated, the discussion chapter will be more difficult than you may have imagined. This chapter requires much hard work and creativity, and thus it, too, takes longer than most students plan for. Furthermore, many students want to finish by a particular deadline, and find that they do not really have as much time as is required. Consequently, many discussion chapters are not as good as they should be. This is unfortunate, because that is the chapter most likely to be read by someone else in the future. You have put much time, money, and hard work into the study and the document; do not lessen that effort by not spending an adequate amount of time on the discussion chapter.

Write abstract. Only when the discussion chapter is finished should you begin the abstract, since the abstract needs to contain information that is in the discussion chapter. The abstract is the most important part of the document in terms of the research community, as it usually will be read before any other part of the document. Remember, you read many abstracts in completing your literature review, and some led you to not read any more of that study.

Preparing for the Final Defense

Beware of those who will not be bothered with details.
William Feather, Sr.

You are ready to undertake many administrative details that many students do not like to do. Furthermore, the nature of these tasks varies from university to university. We will try to identify the most usual procedures, realizing that time frames and requirements may vary.

Make sure that your chair reads and approves the final version. By doing this, you will have the chair backing you. Once approved by your chair, you can set the final defense date and get the room scheduled. Again, Exhibit 7.1 is valuable in getting the committee together. Notice of the final defense probably needs to be given to the graduate school. The final document needs to be distributed to the committee.

TIP: If the requirement is to distribute the document at least 10 working days before the meeting, distribute it 15 or 20 days before the meeting. Your committee will be impressed with you giving them more time. Then check to remind each member about the meeting, and ask if there are any questions or concerns.

TIP: Try to avoid the last possible week for the scheduled defense. Scheduling will be more difficult during this time, and the rush of other last minute students can cause delays on subsequent steps.

Final Defense

The procedures at the final defense are similar to those at the proposal defense, with just a few exceptions. Most final defenses are public meetings, and other students will often be attending (though not to ask questions). Your focus should be on the results and discussion sections--spend as little time as possible discussing the literature review and the study design. Expect a more collegial atmosphere at this meeting than at the proposal defense. Recommended changes will not be made in the study design or hypotheses (since you had a contract on those after the proposal defense), but might be made in the results and discussion chapters. These will ordinarily be cosmetic changes that you can probably make with little effort. Usually the committee will put their trust in the chair to work out those changes with the student.

Following the Final Defense

After the final defense is when the acknowledgements page is written. Whom you thank and what you say is up to you. Usually each committee member is mentioned, significant mentors, family members, and those who have helped you in some way. A maximum of one page should suffice.

Most universities have some required editorial function. You must comply with that function before you can make the requisite number of copies. Signatures from the chair, dean, and other worthy persons may be required. It is appropriate to provide a hardbound copy of your final document to your chair, while soft-bound copies are usually sufficient for the other members of your committee.

Plan to attend commencement! Masters and Doctorates are given special recognition. The exercise is a fitting way to bring closure for most. Family and friends also find this an excellent opportunity to congratulate you on your major academic accomplishment.

Chapter 8

Writing Style

In matters of great importance, style, not sincerity, is the vital thing. **Oscar Wilde**

Be careful of your thoughts; they may become words at any moment. **Iara Gassen**

To base thought only on speech is to try nailing whispers to the wall. Writing freezes thought and offers it up for inspection. **Jack Rosenthal**

Theses and dissertations do not read like novels, newspapers, or even journal articles. They go beyond even the papers that you completed in your various courses. Because these documents are placed in the public domain, they must conform to certain standards. They must report the entire research effort as concisely as possible, while following a particular style manual. This chapter begins with comments about scientific writing style, followed by sections that emphasize various components and the most problematic aspects of those components.

Scientific Writing Style

Theses and dissertations should be as brief as possible, as long as the information is adequately presented. You need to omit your personal prejudices--you need to omit yourself by not using first person personal pronouns. Scientific writhing style differs from general writing style in two major ways--organization and language.

Organization

One of the best ways to concisely communicate is to develop a thorough table of contents before you write anything. The table of contents guides your writing, keeping it in bounds. The table of contents easily identifies to the reader how the material is organized, making it easier to identify omitted material. Provide the reader with summarizing sentences or paragraphs, and transitional sentences providing closure to the previous material and a lead-in to the next material.

All of your decisions should be clearly identified and supported in the literature review chapter. When the decision is made, the reader should be able to say, "Makes sense to me!" These decisions include (a) population, (b) choice of treatment or independent variable, (c) length of treatment, and (d) demographic descriptors.

TIP: In preparing the document, you should:

1. Start with an outline.

2. Write regularly.

3. Write in the same place with dictionary and reference materials nearby.

4. Organize and set priorities.

5. Periodically set the draft aside and take a fresh look in several days.

6. Focus on communication; always keep the reader in mind.

7. Get someone to critique your draft.

8. Be willing to make thorough revisions. (Wilkinson & McNeil, 1996)

Language

Research language appears formal and concise, but it should also flow and keep the reader's interest. Be sure to define any terms that may be unusual or used in a different way in your document (including a section entitled: "Nomenclature" before chapter 1 is a good idea.)

TIP: Students often try to make the document interesting by changing the wording of an often-used word. Synonyms for a major term should not be used, because they lead the reader to believe that new constructs are being introduced.

Past tense is always used, unless (a) referring to a table or a figure, (b) discussing well-established principles, (c) discussing results, (d) discussing conclusions, and (e) discussing the recommendations for future research.

TIP: Writing consists of three stages: planning, writing, and revising. The more time you spend in the planning stage, the less time you will spend in the other two stages.

APA Writing Style

The Publication Manual (APA, 1994) contains both rules about English usage and guides for scientific writing. You will need to keep a copy of it handy while writing, and try "to do it the right way" the first time. Otherwise, you will be compounding your mistakes. These details can occupy much revision time, time that could be spent on other tasks. We present the APA version of some major aspects of various topics, but suggest that you become familiar with whatever style manual you are to use. You need to check with the graduate school to see what their required style is. Do not rely on a recently-finished document.

TIP: Use the index of the style manual often.

Headings

Headings simplify the reading of the document. They should alert the reader when new material is being presented. The headings follow the outline that we encouraged you to develop, initially providing guidance in your literature review and subsequently in your writing.

Chapter headings. Start 1.25 inches from the top of the page. Center "Chapter 1" in boldface. After a double-spaced line, type the chapter title in uppercase entirely, bold, and centered. The chapter heading of this chapter is not in line with these guidelines, as discussed on page 12.

Subheadings. The first level is centered, with major words capitalized. The second level is boldfaced and flush with the left margin, with major words capitalized. The third level is indented (as a paragraph) and is boldfaced and either italicized or underlined, ending with a period.

The text starts after one double-spaced line, and is paragraph-indented (excepting the third level that starts one space after the period). This text reflects this heading structure throughout (with the exception that the beginning of the chapters are not paragraph indented).

Tables

Tables should be placed immediately after being referred to in the text. They should stand alone, without needing the text for clarification. Table numbers and table headings are flush with the left margin, as in Appendix C. The title should concisely identify the elements of the table. Comparable tables should have comparable titles. A solid line is placed under the title heading and under the last line of data. Any notes are described below that line, as in Appendices C and D. Within the text, only refer to highlights of the table, not every element. Capitalize only the first word of all headings in a table.

Notes to a Table

There are three kinds of notes to a table. First, a general note that relates to the table as a whole. It is represented by the word, "Note" (italicized) and is followed by a period. Second, if you want to refer to a specific row, column, or entry, use superscript lowercase letters (see Appendix D). Third, a probability note shows the results of the test of significance, which you would compare with your chosen alpha level. If more than one alpha level is referred to, the largest receives the fewest asterisks (e.g., $*p < .01$ $**p < .001$--see Appendix F).

If more than one of the above kinds of notes are used in one table, order them in the following sequence: general note, specific note, and then probability note, as in Appendix D.

Figures

Figures are usually less preferred than tables as they provide general, approximate information. On the other hand, figures can convey general results much better. Figures are particularly valuable for depicting interactions (see Appendix H) nonlinear relationships (see Appendix I), and procedures (see Exhibit 7.5).

The figure captions should be brief, yet explain what is in the figure.

As with tables, a figure should be understandable without referring to the text. If your figure is reproduced or adapted from another source, you must give credit in the figure caption to the original author and copyright holder (see Exhibit 6.13).

Quotations

Try to use quotes sparingly--only use a quotation if you feel that the quoted material is clearly superior to what you can synthesize with other material. Material that is within quotes (fewer than 40 words), or indented (more than 39 words) requires the author, date, and page number. A block quotation starts on a new line, is indented the same number of spaces as a paragraph, and each subsequent line is flush with the paragraph indent. (See Exhibit 3.3.) The entire block is double-spaced, as is the main document.

By all means make sure that the quotation is accurate. We often find inaccurate quotes, and that is just not professional. There are sometimes legitimate reasons for omitting material, inserting additional material, or adding emphasis--and there are legitimate ways to do this. Whenever you need to modify a quotation, think about restating the material in your own words.

Citations

When referring to published work, give the last name of the author(s) and year of publication. When two or more sources are cited, place them in alphabetical order--not chronological order--as (McNeil & Newman, 1995; Newman, Lewis, & McNeil, 1972). When referring to the McNeil and Newman (1995) article within the text, the parentheses are only around the date, and the ampersand (&) is replaced with the word "and." Subsequent references to a multiple author work, such as "(McNeil, Newman, & Kelly, 1996) are referred to as "(McNeil et al., 1996)." Notice that the "et al." is not italicized and since "et" means "and" there is neither a comma nor a period used. Subsequent references to the same work within the same paragraph do not require the date.

Numbers

Numbers nine and under are spelled out. Occasions when numbers under 10 are not spelled out:

1. When a number appears in the same sentence with numbers above nine, referring to the same category, as "there were 6 toys, 8 boxes, and 13 cards."

2. Measurements of time (3 hours) or space (6 square miles).

3. Percentages are expressed as numerals: 16% and 3%. When the numeral is unspecified, use "percentage."

Sentences should not begin with a numeral, but we find "Twenty-six participants were . . ." to be awkward. Reword the sentence, "Of the total participants, 26 were . . ."

Statistical Symbols

All statistical symbols are italicized, except X^2. This includes t, F, r, df, R^2, p, z, N, n, M, and SD. N is the total sample size, whereas n is the size of a particular group. M represents the mean and SD represents the standard deviation.

Spelling and Punctuation

The Publication Manual (APA, 1994) contains spelling and grammar guidelines. Errors that occur often are the following:

1. Percent is spelled as one word and used with numerals. Percentage is a noun.

2. In seriation, use a comma before the word "and": "x, y, and z"--not "x, y and z."

3. The dash is either an em dash (longer than a dash)--or two dashes as just presented, with no space on either side or between the two dashes.

4. "1990s" has no apostrophe.

5. "July 4, 1996" or "July 1996" or "4 July 1996."

6. Hyphens are used

   a. when self is used as a prefix.

   b. two words form a single idea, such as "one-third vote."

   c. a prefix modifies a capitalized word: "post-Modern."

   d. a numeral follows a prefix: "pre-1990."

   e. an abbreviation is used: "post-APA certification."

   f. more than one word is a modifier: "Second-degree relationship."

   g. word would be misread: "co-worker" rather than "coworker."

7. Place commas after these Latin abbreviations: "e.g.," "i.e.," "etc."

8. Do not use a colon between a verb and its object or a preposition and its object: "The objectives are as follows:" not "The objectives are:" "The study:" not "The study was designed to:"

9. Seasons are not capitalized: "spring" not "Spring."

10. In titles and headings--all words of four or more letters are capitalized.

11. Both parts of a hyphenated compound are capitalized: "Pre-Kindergarten" and "Self-Assessment."

Latin Abbreviations

Spacing, use of periods, and use of commas are often incorrectly used in Latin abbreviations. The four most commonly used Latin abbreviations are the following:

1. "i.e." meaning "that is"--followed by a comma

2. "e.g." meaning "for example"--followed by a comma

3. "etc." meaning "and so forth"--followed by a comma

4. "cf." meaning "compare"

Chapter 9

Research Time Lines

Conducting research is a very involved process, and one that can be very threatening at first. Both statements led to the suggestion that a time line be developed, one that not only shows what must be done, but the order in which it must be done, and the approximate amount of time that it will take. We provide several checklists in this chapter to accomplish these goals.

Standard Amount of Time

We first present the estimated amount of time for each of the large sections of a thesis or dissertation. We follow this with a detailed time line condensed to two semesters. Frequently two semesters is not sufficient, although our experience is that most students think that they can finish in just two semesters. As you can see in Exhibit 9.1, data collection and data analysis, and writing take the most months. These are average estimates, and as such there will be variations from student to student. Usually, though, any task is going to take longer than you estimate.

Exhibit 9.1. Estimates (in months) for completing a thesis or dissertation.

Topic search and proposal	3
Literature review	2
Data collection and analysis	5
Writing and editing	6
Total months	16

Exhibit 9.2 contains a more detailed listing of the various tasks, if you want to finish the entire process in two semesters. The time line is tight; thus, slipping on the due date for any one activity is going to make it tougher to meet the deadlines for the subsequent tasks. One thing that students often are not aware of are the required activities after the defense, and the amount of time those activities take.

Exhibit 9.2. Two semester time line for completing a thesis or dissertation.

Date finished	Weeks	Activity accomplished
9/7	2	Pick chair and review format
9/25	4	Topic search
9/15	2	Committee chosen
10/25	8	Literature review
11/15	4	Proposal development and defense
12/15	5	Collect data
2/1	5	Analyze data
4/1	8	Write chapter 4 and 5, and revise chapter 1-3
4/15	1	Oral defense
5/1	1	Final revision to required location
5/10	1	Graduation

Specific Time Line

There are at least two ways to think about a specific time line. One way is to picture the blocks of activities that need to be accomplished and how they relate to one another. That is best communicated as a PERT (Program Evaluation and Review Technique, Cook, 1966) chart as in Exhibit 9.3. The arrows in Exhibit 9.3 show the flow of the activities. Therefore, the activities that are at the beginning of the arrow must be completed before the activities at the end of the arrow can be started.

Another way to think of all the activities is to list them in detail; then check them off as they are completed. This process allows for more detail than would be feasible in the PERT chart in Exhibit 9.3. There are two disadvantages of listing all the activities in Exhibit 9.4. First, not all studies will require all of the activities. We have tried to show this by including the two categories of "required" and "optional." All researchers will need to do all of the required tasks, whereas you will need to decide if you, your chair, your committee, or your research will require the optional tasks. While the entire list of tasks may seem overpowering at this time, it is better to identify them now than try to attempt to accomplish them after it is too late.

Exhibit 9.3. PERT chart of research activities.

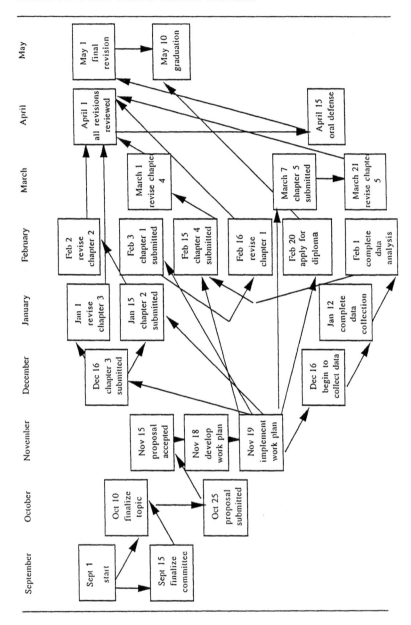

Exhibit 9.4. Detailed list of research activities.

Required	Optional	Activity
_x_	___	Select chair
_x_	___	Focus on topic
___	_x_	Get advice from chair on other members
_x_	___	Select committee
___	_x_	Talk with committee about their specialty
_x_	___	Identify treatment (or IV) in literature
_x_	___	Write up treatment in literature review
_x_	___	Identify outcomes (or DV) from literature
_x_	___	Verify outcome measure is available
_x_	___	Complete Human Participants Clearance Form
___	_x_	Get chair ok on consent form
___	_x_	Get chair ok on instructions to participants
___	_x_	Get preliminary ok from participants
___	_x_	Train assistants
___	_x_	Run pilot studies
___	_x_	Plan for data analysis
___	_x_	Draft data analysis plan
___	_x_	Construct table shells
___	_x_	Meet periodically with chair
___	_x_	Get proposal ok from chair
___	_x_	Attend another proposal defense
_x_	___	Set date for defense of proposal
_x_	___	Distribute proposal
___	_x_	Check: did all committee receive proposal?
___	_x_	Ask committee if any problems
___	_x_	Remind committee of place and date
___	_x_	Discuss with chair the proposal defense
___	_x_	Prepare for proposal defense
___	_x_	Arrange for note-taking during defense
_x_	___	Defend proposal
___	_x_	Write memo regarding changes
___	_x_	Enlist participants
___	_x_	Contact institution regarding data collection

(Exhibit continues)

Required	Optional	Activity
_x_	____	Obtain multiple copies of instrument(s)
_x_	____	Collect data
_x_	____	Store data in secure location
____	_x_	Code data
____	_x_	Enter data
____	_x_	Verify data entry
____	_x_	Make preliminary runs to check accuracy
_x_	____	Analyze data
_x_	____	Construct tables
_x_	____	Write chapter 4 (results)
____	_x_	Include summary table at end of chapter 4
_x_	____	Write chapter 5 (discussion)
_x_	____	Write abstract
_x_	____	Finalize tables and appendices
____	_x_	Feedback to participants
____	_x_	Get chair approval of entire document
_x_	____	Copy document
_x_	____	Set defense date
_x_	____	Distribute copies
____	_x_	Remind committee of date
____	_x_	Check for concerns
_x_	____	Final defense
_x_	____	Make corrections
_x_	____	Get approval from chair
____	_x_	Write acknowledgements page
_x_	____	Work with designated editor
_x_	____	Clearance from editor
_x_	____	Get required signatures
_x_	____	Turn in final copy
_x_	____	Make sure all fees paid
_x_	____	Make sure all forms filled out
____	_x_	Attend commencement

Content Checklist

Another way to check your research is to make a final content check of the material in the document. Is the document communicating what you are supposed to communicate? Exhibit 9.5 contains a list of questions that you may want to ask yourself, or have a colleague respond to. Again, not all institutions will be expecting the same material in each chapter, but these are generalities.

Exhibit 9.5. Content checklist.

Chapter 1.
Is the problem stated in a general way?
Is the purpose related to the problem?
Are the questions or hypotheses related to the problem and the purpose?
Is the rationale clear, and indicative of a general way for the study to proceed?
Is there a focus at the end of the chapter?
Is there a transition to Chapter 2?
Chapter 2.
Does it appear that the literature was reviewed comprehensively and critically?
Does the review explain what is known and how the present study will expand on that knowledge?
Are the headings clear, and are there transitions from one section to the next?
Is each major section summarized, and is there a final summary of the entire chapter?
Is there a transition to chapter 3?
Chapter 3.
Is there a rationale for the demographic information?
Are the procedures specified clearly and thoroughly enough so that the study could be replicated?
Are all the variables called for in the literature review?
Are all the variables clearly operationally defined?
Is the setting of the study described such that an outsider would realize how it relates to their setting?

(Exhibit continues)

Are the instructions to participants included?

Is the consent form adequate and included?

Is the treatment long enough to have an observable effect?

Is the sample size large enough to obtain significance?

Are participant selection criteria specified?

Is the response rate identified, and information provided about why there might not have been a 100% response rate?

Is there a transition to chapter 4?

Chapter 4.

Are demographic descriptive statistics of the sample presented?

Can the tables be read easily, and are they all necessary?

Does the reporting of results flow (results by research hypothesis usually help the flow)?

If results are from after-the-fact hypotheses, is that clear?

Are just the facts presented in chapter 4?

Is there a transition to chapter 5?

Chapter 5.

Are the results discussed in relation to the knowledge base?

Are the delimitations of the study related to the results?

Are limitations of the data related to the results?

Are the results discussed in a non-biased fashion--providing alternative interpretations of the results?

Are the suggestions for further research clearly implied from the study, or could they have been stated before the study was conducted?

Does the summary highlight only the important aspects of the research?

After parts.

Are all of the cited references included in the references?

Do the references follow the style manual?

Are all the tables readable?

Are all the necessary forms in the appendices (including Human Participants Clearance Form, consent form, and crucial communications with participants and their institutions)?

Has the anonymity of participants been honored in the main document and the after parts?

References

American Psychological Association. (1994). *Publication manual of the American Psychological Association.* Washington, DC: Author.

Campbell, D. T., & Stanley, J. C. (1963). *Experimental and quasi experimental designs for research.* Chicago: Rand McNally.

Cook, D. L. (1966). *Program evaluation review technique applications in education.* Washington, DC: US Government Printing Office.

Kerlinger, F. N. (1986). *Foundations of behavioral research* (3rd ed.). New York: Holt, Rinehart, & Winston.

McNeil, K., & Phillips, B. N. (1968). Dear teacher: This is an attempt to interpret some research findings. *Psychology in the Schools, 5,* 361-364.

Newman, I., & Newman, C. (1994). *Conceptual statistics for beginners* (2nd ed.). Lanham, MD: University Press of America.

Wilkinson, W., & McNeil, K. (1996). *Research for the helping professions.* Pacific Grove, CA: Brooks/Cole.

APPENDIX A

Example of Means and Subgroups

Table 1

Mean Item Score for the 149 Offense
Descriptions by Gender and Racial Groups

Group	*n*	*M*
Males only	29	6.56
Females only	28	5.53
Whites only	36	6.02
Blacks only	21	6.10
White males	20	6.43
White females	16	5.52
Black males	9	6.85
Black females	12	5.54

APPENDIX B

Example of Reporting Demographic Results on Instrument

PLEASE FILL IN THE BLANKS BEFORE
YOU COMPLETE THIS QUESTIONNAIRE

AGE   26.51   SEX   Male (51%) Female (49%)

EDUCATIONAL LEVEL 13.51 RACE White (63%) Black (37%)

APPROXIMATE INCOME PER YEAR:

0 to $2,999	23%
$3,000 to $5,999	30%
$6,000 to $9,999	19%
$10,000 to $13,999	18%
Above $14,000	11%

ARE YOU IN A POSITION TO HIRE A NEW EMPLOYEE?

YES 5%

NO 95%

DO YOU BELIEVE THAT SOMEDAY YOU WILL BE IN A
POSITION TO HIRE A NEW EMPLOYEE?

YES 46%

NO 19%

UNSURE 35%

Note. A total of 57 people responded to the Continuum of Criminal
Offense Questionnaire.

APPENDIX C

Reporting of Means and Standard Deviations by Categories

Table 1

Means and Standard Deviations of Offense Rating as a Function of Type of Harm Inflicted on Victims and Legal Classification of Main Offense for Class I Category Offenses with over $250 Taken

Legal classification of main offense	Number of offenses considered	Type of harm inflicted on victim			
		None	Minor	Hospitalization	Death
Criminal homicide	2				10.40
Robbery Gunpoint or knifepoint	3	6.91 (1.89)	7.22 (2.02)	9.15 (1.43)	
Robbery Blunt instrument	3	6.34 (2.03)	7.09 (2.04)	7.42 (2.08)	
Robbery Physical force	3	6.09 (1.95)	6.95 (1.94)	7.56 (1.95)	
Robbery Verbal assault	3	6.06 (1.99)			

Note. The numbers within the parentheses are the standard deviations. The Continuum of Criminal Offenses Questionnaire contains a scale that ranges from 1 (least serious offense rating) through 11 (most serious offense rating).

APPENDIX D

Reliability Information

Table 2

Cronbach's Coefficient Alpha Reliability for the Psychological Screening Inventory

| | | Psychological Screening Inventory | | | | | |
Group	*n*	Al[a] (24)	Sn[b] (25)	Di[c] (30)	Ex[d] (30)	De[e] (20)	Total (129)
"Accepted" pretrial intervention offender males and females	71	.54	.72	.86	.59	.51	.70
"Accepted" pretrial intervention offender males	43	.48	.73	.87	.62	.53	.73
"Accepted" pretrial intervention offender females	28	.62	.65	.82	.51	.49	.65
Non-Offender males	32	.56	.70	.84	.53	.38	.62

Note. Cronbach's Coefficient Alpha gives an estimate of internal consistency.

[a]Al is the abbreviation for the Alienation Scale.
[b]Sn is the abbreviation for the Social-Conformity Scale.
[c]Di is an abbreviation for the Discomfort Scale.
[d]Ex is an abbreviation for the Expression Scale.
[e]De is an abbreviation for the Defensiveness Scale.

APPENDIX E

Summary Table for Regression Results

Table 4

Summary Table of Models Tested, R^2 Values, F Ratios, and Significance Levels for Testing Differences Between the "Accepted" Pretrial Intervention Offender Group and the Non-Offender Group on Selected Psycho-Social Variables

Hypothesis Number	Models Tested	R^2_f	R^2_r	df	F	p	Significant
1	1 vs. 99	.00	.00	1/166	.81	.37	NS
2	2 vs. 99	.09	.00	1/166	16.06	.01	S
3	3 vs. 99	.00	.00	1/166	.03	.87	NS
4	4 vs. 99	.00	.00	1/166	.88	.35	NS
5	5 vs. 99	.01	.00	1/166	1.41	.24	NS
6	6 vs. 99	.00	.00	1/166	.47	.50	NS
7	7 vs. 99	.01	.00	1/166	1.14	.29	NS
8	8 vs. 99	.00	.00	1/166	.05	.82	NS
9	9 vs. 99	.00	.00	1/166	.44	.51	NS
10	10 vs. 99	.01	.00	1/166	1.57	.21	NS
11	11 vs. 99	.00	.00	1/166	2.20	.14	NS
12	12 vs. 99	.01	.00	1/166	1.30	.25	NS
13	13 vs. 99	.00	.00	1/166	.64	.42	NS
14	14 vs. 99	.00	.00	1/166	.01	.93	NS
15	15 vs. 99	.03	.00	1/166	5.50	.02	S
16	16 vs. 99	.00	.00	1/166	.11	.74	NS
17	17 vs. 99	.00	.00	1/166	.24	.63	NS

Note. See Table C for a complete statement of the specific research hypotheses tested. Alpha was .05, however, when the correction for multiple comparisons was used, a .025 probability level had to be obtained. S = Significant. NS = Not Significant.

APPENDIX F

Example of Results for Two Groups

Table 3

Mean, Median, Range, Standard Deviation, and Variance Calculated on the EDS (n = 15) for the Two Pilot Samples

EDS score	Master's level students		Pretrial offenders	
	n	*%*	*n*	*%*
15 - 16	0	0	0	0
12 - 14	0	0	0	0
9 - 11	0	0	1	12
6 - 8	0	0	6	75
3 - 5	3	43	0	0
0 - 2	4	57	1	12
Total	7	100	8	100
M	2.71		6.18	
Median	2.00		6.00	
Range	0 - 5		1 - 10	
SD	1.47		2.32	
SD^2	2.16		5.38	
t		-3.54*		

* Significant at the .01 level for a two-tailed test.

APPENDIX G

Correlation Matrix

Table 5

Intercorrelations Between Scores (n = 65)

Variable	2	3	4	5	6	7
1 Denial	.38	.15	.05	-.34	.42	-.11
2 Anger		.31	.13	-.37	.59	-.17
3 Bargaining			-.06	-.04	.56	-.11
4 Depression				.13	.51	.31
5 Acceptance					.25	.08
6 Alpha-Omega Total						-.01

Note. All correlations are rounded off to the nearest hundredth decimal point. A correlation coefficient of .34 or higher is significant at the .05 level, and a correlation coefficient of .48 or higher is significant at the .01 level. Variables 1 through 6 come from the Alpha-Omega Completed Sentence Form. Variable 7 (Stress) comes from the Social Readjustment Rating Scale.

APPENDIX H

An Example of an Interaction Figure

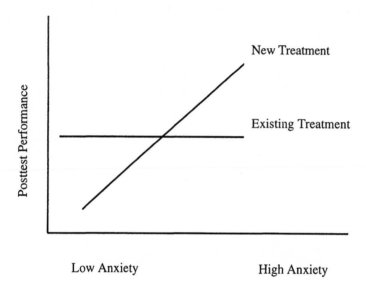

Figure 1. The expected interaction between anxiety and treatment on posttest performance.

APPENDIX I

An Example of a Nonlinear Relationship

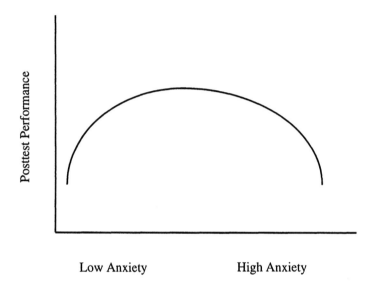

Figure 2. The expected nonlinear relationship between anxiety and posttest performance.

Index

Isadore Newman received his PhD in educational psychology with a specialty in statistics and measurement from Southern Illinois University at Carbondale in 1971. He has been a professor at the University of Akron since 1971. During his professional career, he has served on over 300 dissertation committees and has presented hundreds of papers at state, national, and international meetings. He has written 9 books and monographs and has served on many editorial boards, in addition to being the editor of *Multiple Linear Regression Viewpoints* and the *Midwestern Educational Researcher*. He is the primary author on another popular text published by University Press of America: *Conceptual Statistics for Beginners*.

Carolyn R. Benz received her PhD in education at the University of Akron in 1980 after which she remained there as an institutional researcher for nine years. She served as Assistant Professor in the Department of Educational Administration there for one year and was an Associate Professor at the University of Hartford. She has been a faculty member at the University of Dayton since 1990, achieving the rank of Professor in 1997. She teaches doctoral research methodology courses, both quantitative and qualitative, as well as the dissertation proposal writing seminar. She has coauthored two previous books.

David Weis is a Professor of Education at the University of Akron. He is the chair of the Department of Counseling and Special Education and is a Senior Fellow in the Institute for Life-Span Development and Gerontology. He is also the Training Director of the Education College's program for Counseling Psychology.

Keith McNeil received his PhD in educational psychology from the University of Texas at Austin in 1967. He began teaching at Southern Illinois University at Carbondale that year. He ran his own consulting business for 2 years, worked in a state department of education for 1 year, worked 8 years on a federal contract providing evaluation assistance to state and local educational agencies, and worked for 5 years as an evaluator in the Dallas public schools. He rejoined higher education in 1989 at New Mexico State University, where he teaches statistics, research design, and the dissertation writing course. He recently coauthored *Research for the Helping Professions* and *Testing Research Hypotheses with the General Linear Model*.